The
Fish & Seafood
Cookbook

The Fish & Seafood Cookbook

FROM OCEAN TO TABLE

CONSULTANT EDITORS
SUSANNA TEE AND FIONA BIGGS

This edition published in 2010
LOVE FOOD is an imprint of Parragon Books Ltd

Parragon
Queen Street House
4 Queen Street
Bath BA1 1HE, UK

ISBN: 978-1-4454-0362-5

Printed in China

Internal Design by Talking Design
Edited by Fiona Biggs and Susanna Tee
Photography by Clive Streeter
Illustrations by Coral Mula
Food styling by Angela Drake, Teresa Goldfinch and
Emma Jane Frost

The Marine Conservation Society (MCS) is the UK charity dedicated
to protecting our seas, shores and wildlife.

Please join us – visit our website at www.mcsuk.org
Make a difference – choose sustainable seafood www.fishonline.org
Reg Charity No (England and Wales) 1004005
Reg Charity No (Scotland) SC037480
Company Limited by Guarantee (England & Wales) No: 2550966
Registered Office: Unit 3, Wolf Business Park, Alton Road,
Ross-on-Wye HR9 5NB
Tel: 01989 566017
VAT No. 489 1505 17

NOTES FOR THE READER

This book uses both metric and imperial measurements. Follow
the same units of measurement throughout; do not mix metric
and imperial. All spoon measurements are level: teaspoons are
assumed to be 5 ml, and tablespoons are assumed to be 15 ml.

Unless otherwise stated, milk is assumed to be full fat, eggs and
individual vegetables are medium, and pepper is freshly ground
black pepper.
The times given are an approximate guide only. Preparation
times differ according to the techniques used by different people
and the cooking times may also vary from those given. Optional
ingredients, variations or serving suggestions have not been
included in the calculations.
Recipes using raw or very lightly cooked eggs should be avoided
by infants, the elderly, pregnant women, convalescents and
anyone suffering from an illness. Pregnant and breastfeeding
women are advised to avoid eating peanuts and peanut products.
Sufferers from nut allergies should be aware that some of the
ready-made ingredients used in the recipes in this book may
contain nuts. Always check the packaging before use.

Picture Acknowledgements

The publisher would like to thank the following for permission to
reproduce copyright material on the following pages: 8, 11, 12
and 14 (Bryce Beukers-Stewart), 13 and 15 (Peter Richardson),
and front cover (sardines © Image Source/Getty Images).

MCS recognizes that many stocks of our favourite fish species
are overfished and unsustainable, and appear on our Fish
to Avoid list. However, MCS also highlights the stocks of
these species that are in a healthier state and provide a more
sustainable option. When buying your seafood use the MCS
Pocket Good Fish Guide (downloadable from www.mcsuk.
org) to find the most sustainable option for your favourite
seafood.

CONTENTS

FRESHWATER FISH   114

SHELLFISH   142

INTRODUCTION

The *Fish & Seafood cookbook* is a comprehensive guide to preparing, cooking and serving every kind of fish and shellfish. Confirmed fish devotees will be delighted to have all their favourite, classic recipes in one volume, together with a range of new, and imaginative ideas, while those who may find fish preparation rather daunting will be enlightened, reassured and inspired.

The Fish Directories at the front of chapters one to five introduce the fabulous wealth of healthy, delicious food that our waters – both fresh and sea – can offer. All the basic techniques for preparing and cooking these different varieties of fish and shellfish are then explained and demonstrated in detail.The collection of recipes that follows caters for every meal type and occasion, from elegant finger food to hearty main meals, and encompasses all the popular cuisines around the globe, from the Mediterranean to Mexico.

AN INTRODUCTION TO THE MARINE CONSERVATION SOCIETY

 **Marine Conservation Society**

The Marine Conservation Society (MCS) is the UK charity dedicated to the protection of our seas, shores and the wildlife that depends on them. MCS campaigns for clean seas and beaches, sustainable fisheries, protection of marine life and their habitats, and the sensitive use of our marine resources for future generations.

What MCS does

The coastal and marine environments of the UK are some of the most beautiful in the world, supporting an astonishing diversity of habitats and species, as well as providing vital resources for economic development, food and recreation. However, our coastal habitats are under increasing pressure from development, tourism and climate change, while further offshore, marine habitats and species are threatened by activities associated with fisheries, aggregate extraction and offshore energy developments.

Through education and community involvement – from marine-life surveys to beach cleans and litter surveys – and collaboration, MCS helps to raise awareness of the many threats that face our marine environment and promotes various types of action at individual, industry and government level to ensure that our seas are fit for life and will remain so in the future.

Fishing for the future

Healthy fish stocks are a vital part of the marine ecosystem, and provide protein and livelihoods for billions of people. Globally, fisheries supply over 2.9 billion people with at least 15 per cent of their average protein intake.

Overfishing is a significant and growing threat to marine biodiversity and many fish stocks are widely reported to be in a state of serious decline. As well as reducing stocks and ultimately affecting the livelihoods of those working in the industry, the methods used can also have devastating impacts on habitats and non-target species such as dolphins, marine turtles and birds, as a result of dredging and by-catch.

Annually, 51.7 metric tonnes – 47 per cent of the seafood destined for dinner tables worldwide – are currently produced by fish farms. Increasing global demand for fish and the limited quantity of wild fish stocks mean that fish-farm production is expected to double by 2030. After Chile and Norway, the UK is the third largest producer of farmed Atlantic salmon.

By raising awareness of the issues surrounding fishing and fish farming and promoting sustainable seafood consumption, MCS aims to encourage more sustainable fisheries management and practices, securing a long-term future for our fisheries and marine environment.

Protection of marine habitat and species

Although the UK's seas support a variety of life as fascinating and colourful as that found anywhere in the world, providing a home for over 8,000 species, we know very little about the marine environment.

Consequently, protection of marine habitats and species has not kept pace with that of our terrestrial landscapes and wildlife, and our activities are wreaking damage on a significant scale. The MCS Biodiversity Programme uses surveys, education and policy development to ensure that marine species and habitats are afforded protection before it's too late. The programme includes:

• the study of rare yet important species
• campaigning for sanctuaries for marine life – marine reserves – where nothing can be done that would damage marine life. At present only 0.0009 per cent of the UK's seas are protected by two small marine reserves, one at Lundy Island, and one in Lamlash Bay on the Isle of Arran

- campaigning for the introduction of new marine laws to protect marine wildlife and habitats and to ensure the sustainable management of seas and resources
- engaging in vital marine turtle conservation and research and supporting turtle conservation projects around the world.

Pollution-free seas

Toxic chemicals, sewage, crude oil, radioactive waste, agricultural fertilizers, animal waste, storm run-off from our city streets and millions of tonnes of litter all threaten our seas and shoreline. Pollution can contaminate the fish we eat, the water in which we swim and the beaches we visit.

For over 20 years MCS has campaigned in the UK for clean seas and beaches, encouraging everyone to take an active role to prevent further damage.

Community action for clean seas and beaches

Walk along a UK beach and, on average, you'll find 2,000 pieces of litter per kilometre. Beach litter is now a global problem that has a major impact on wildlife, and costs the UK millions of pounds annually in clean-up costs.

MCS has run the Adopt-A-Beach and Beachwatch campaigns since 1993, involving thousands of volunteers in beach cleans and litter surveys every year. It has been able to target specific sources of litter, influence government policy and industry practices, helping to develop solutions to this modern environmental hazard.

The annual MCS *Good Beach Guide* aims to stop the dumping of raw sewage at sea by promoting beaches with the best water quality,

recommending beaches that we think are now clean enough for swimming. There's only one charity in the UK that cares for all of our seas, shores and wildlife – MCS. MCS works for sustainable fisheries, clean seas and beaches, protection of marine life and the sensitive use

of our marine resources so that they will benefit future generations. Everyone, from individuals to businesses, can support MCS – please go to www.mcsuk.org or contact MCS (see page 4 of this book for contact details).

WHY BUY ECO-FRIENDLY FISH?

Overfishing and stock depletion

The impact of overfishing on fish stocks and the wider marine environment is an issue of growing global concern. A greater demand for fish as world populations increase and people become aware of the health benefits of eating fish, and other influences such as climate change, are also all contributing to overfishing.

For example, Atlantic cod is listed as a threatened and declining species in the Greater North and Celtic Seas. In the North Sea the stock has declined by 75 per cent since the 1970s. A plan is now in place to allow stocks to recover, although catches must remain low in order to allow recovery to take place. However, only about 30 per cent of the cod landed by UK vessels into the UK and abroad is caught in the North Sea. Most of the rest of the cod eaten in Britain is imported from areas such as the

Eco-friendly fish is fish that is caught in such a way as to have no harmful effect on the stock, the marine environment or other species. By choosing only fish from healthy, responsibly managed sources, caught using methods that minimize damage to the marine environment and other species, consumers can help drive the market for sustainably produced seafood and make a real difference to the way our fish stocks are managed.

Barents and Norwegian Seas, where stocks are more sustainably managed. Landings of haddock, whiting and saithe from the North Sea have all declined since the 1970s and 1980s; indeed, North Sea mackerel has never recovered from the collapse of the fishery in the 1970s and the closures remain in place to protect the stock.

The common skate, paradoxically, is now becoming very rare in UK shallow seas and in European waters.

The situation in the North Sea, however, has to be balanced with a more positive situation in other UK fisheries, for example in the waters off the southwest coast of England, where there is an increasing understanding of, and a progression towards, more sustainable fisheries.

Impact of fishing on marine species and habitat

Every year hundreds of thousands of marine mammals, turtles and seabirds are killed needlessly in fishing gears all over the world. In many cases these deaths could be avoided, or at least reduced, by introducing the use of 'dolphin-', 'turtle-' and 'seabird-friendly' devices, or by banning the use of damaging practices and by introducing areas in which fishing is prohibited. Similarly, in fisheries where by-catch of seabirds, especially albatross, is problematic, simple practical measures have been devised

to help prevent seabirds being hooked and drowned on longlines.

The most widely used and energy-intensive of all fishing methods is trawling. Examples of fishing methods that directly affect the seabed are bottom trawling, beam trawling and dredging. Depending on the nature of the seabed in which these gears are used, the damage to fragile habitats such as cold-water corals and seamounts can be substantial and irreversible. By restricting their use to areas where the seabed is less sensitive and by adopting measures to reduce the negative impacts associated with them, these fishing methods can be made more sustainable.

Socio-economic consequences

The majority of global catch comes from the waters of developing countries where local inhabitants rely heavily on seafood as a main source of animal protein. As the overfishing crisis in waters of developed countries deepens and demand for fish intensifies, there is increasing pressure on the fishery resources of developing countries. In Europe, for example, a significant proportion of the fish consumed is imported from developing countries. Meanwhile, in the UK, as a result of the industrialization of fisheries and overfishing, the number of fishermen has reduced by 47 per cent in recent years, from 23,990 in 1981 to 12,729 in 2007, leaving once vibrant and bustling harbours lying idle.

Fish farming

Fish farming is often suggested as the solution to the rising demand for fish. Done well it is part of the solution, done badly it is part of the problem. In the UK, marine fish such as salmon and cod are transferred as juveniles from hatcheries to sea pens or cages where they are grown on to harvest size. The pens are suspended in the sea in inshore waters and have a constant flow of water through them. The fish are fed either by hand or by using automated feed systems. All waste and, in some instances, uneaten feed falls through the bottom of the cages to the seabed below. The cages can be damaged during storms or by accidents, which can lead to fish escaping, causing problems for depleted wild salmon stocks as a result of interbreeding and increased competition for food.

MCS Sustainable Seafood Programme

MCS has raised the profile of several important fisheries issues, including 'no take zones' or the introduction of marine reserves to protect fish stocks and habitat, the unsustainability of deep-water fisheries and, most recently, the consumers' role in making environmentally informed choices about the fish they eat, thus increasing support for sustainable fisheries. As the overfishing crisis deepens, the need for the education of consumers to increase demand for responsibly produced seafood has become ever more important.

Fishonline.org

Following the publication of the *Good Fish Guide* in 2002, MCS launched **www.fishonline.org** in August 2004. The website provides information on over 150 species of fish and shellfish, advice on the status of individual species and/or stocks and a rating based on their relative sustainability. The website also features a list of Fish to Eat and Fish to Avoid, based on the ratings applied through the Fishonline system. You can also download the most up-to-date version of the MCS Pocket Good Fish Guide, which can be used when out and about, whether eating at a restaurant or doing the weekly shop.

INCREASING THE SUSTAINABILITY OF THE FISH YOU EAT

Consumers can make a real difference to the way our fish stocks are managed. When deciding which fish to eat, consider what it is, where it was caught and how.

Biology and life history
Avoid eating species that are long-lived, slow-growing, late to mature and therefore vulnerable to overfishing. Examples of these types of fish include orange roughy, sharks, skates and some species of ray.

Seasonality
Avoid eating fish during their breeding season. Details of when fish breed are available at the MCS website **www.fishonline.org.**

Size and maturity
Size matters! Avoid eating immature, small, undersized fish and shellfish that have not yet had the chance to reproduce or breed. For more information on the size at which many fish species mature, go to **www.fishonline.org.**

Stock status
Avoid eating fish from depleted stocks. When buying fish you need to be aware that, while certain species are overfished in one area, the situation may not be as bad in another, for example haddock (overfished in the West of Scotland and Faroe Islands but sustainable from the Northeast Artic).

Fishing method
Where possible, choose the most selective or sustainable fishing method available. When choosing haddock for example, which is generally fished together with cod, whiting and saithe, choose line-caught fish as this reduces the number of cod taken as by-catch. This is especially important where the cod stock is depleted.

Know what you are eating
Often fish is labelled with the generic or family name for the species, for example tuna. There are seven commercially available species of tuna, three of which are listed by the World Conservation Union (IUCN). Big-eye has been assessed as vulnerable; Northern bluefin as endangered in the East

Atlantic and critically endangered in the West Atlantic and is also listed by Oslo/Paris Convention (OSPAR) as a threatened and declining species; and Southern bluefin is assessed as critically endangered. Also yellowfin tuna is listed as least concern and albacore is listed as vulnerable in the North Atlantic and critically endangered in the South Atlantic.

Look at the label

Look for seafood products bearing the Marine Stewardship Council (MSC) label – The Fish with the Blue Tick. The role of the MSC is to recognize well managed fisheries, via a certification programme, and to harness consumer purchasing power to promote environmentally responsible fisheries. See **www.msc.org** for information.

Farmed fish

When eating farmed fish such as trout, carp and warm water prawns, look out for the organic label. Scottish rope-grown mussels are a good choice as the methods used in their production have little environmental impact.

US-farmed catfish are also a good choice in terms of sustainability, as they are farmed in closed inland ponds using re-circulating freshwater, both of which processes prevent escapes and disease transfer. Catfish are also fed a primarily vegetarian diet, which reduces pressure on wild fish caught for fish-feed production.

Lobsters, while not farmed, can be ranched or enhanced. In Cornwall, the National Lobster Hatchery at Padstow releases 5–10,000 juvenile lobsters each year to boost wild stocks and to maintain a sustainable fishery for this species. Tagging or V-notching schemes have also

been adopted on a regional basis to protect egg-bearing female lobsters. V-notching is the removal of a small piece of tail segment from the tail of an egg-bearing or 'berried' lobster which, if caught, is returned to the sea to continue breeding.

Organic

The organic label applies only to farmed seafood, as only the production of farmed fish can be controlled. The main certification body in the UK, the Soil Association, currently certifies a range of species, including salmon and trout, while standards for other species are under development. Other organic seafood products available in the UK, such as warm water prawns, are certified by other European bodies such as Naturland in Germany.

Organic farming practices meet high environmental standards, including strict limits and restrictions on the use of medicines, chemicals and sea-lice treatments. Feed is sourced sustainably and the number of fish in the cages is generally fewer than on non-organic farms.

Freedom Food certification

Freedom Food is a scheme run by the RSPCA to ensure high welfare standards are implemented and maintained for farmed animals.

A set of standards has been developed for farmed salmon that is based around the Farm Animal Welfare Council's five principles:
• freedom to express normal behaviour
• freedom from fear and distress
• freedom from hunger and malnutrition
• freedom from discomfort and pain
• freedom from injury and disease.

BUYING AND STORING FISH

Buying

Freshness is the all-important factor to consider when buying any seafood that hasn't been preserved for long-term storage. Fresh fish is highly perishable so, unless you have access to supplies as they are landed, much of the 'fresh' fish for sale will have been frozen on the fishing vessel and then thawed. It is vitally important for you to know the signs of fish in prime condition and those specimens that you should avoid.

Whether you are buying your seafood at a supermarket's fish counter, from a fishmonger or from a market stall, the display slab should be spotlessly clean and there should be plenty of crushed ice around the seafood. Whole, gutted fish deteriorate less quickly than steaks or fillets, so look for a display that includes these.

Your nose will give you the first indication of what you should or shouldn't buy. Good-quality fish has a fresh, ocean-like aroma. It shouldn't smell 'fishy'. If there is any whiff of ammonia or unpleasantness, don't buy. The odour is caused by bacteria rapidly multiplying as the fish deteriorates.

Whole fish should be firm, not floppy, and the flesh should feel firm and elastic when you press gently. The eyes should be protruding and clear, not sunken or cloudy; any scales should be shiny and tight against the skin; the gills should be clear and bright red, not dull or grey. Fillets and steaks should be cleanly cut and look moist and fresh, with a shiny 'bloom' on the surface and no yellowing or browning.

Never buy packaged fish with damaged packaging. There should not be much air between the fish and the wrapping or any pools of liquid or blood. And, of course, you should check the use-by date.

The term 'shellfish' includes a wide range of specimens – bivalves (clams, mussels, oysters, scallops), crustaceans (crabs, lobsters, prawns) and cephalopods (squid and octopus) – they should all be consumed on the day of purchase.

When clams, mussels and oysters are sold alive, the shells should be tightly closed; if open shells don't snap shut when tapped, they are dead. They should be in a net or porous bag, not a polythene bag. Most scallops are sold shucked, often with the roe attached, but

occasionally in the shell. Shrimp and Dublin Bay prawns are often sold frozen, but can also be raw or cooked. It is best to buy them in the shell – look for firm flesh, and avoid any with black spots on the shells (except in the case of large black tiger prawns). Squid and octopus are both sold fresh and frozen – the flesh shouldn't have any brown patches. Both smell foul if not fresh.

Make sure the packaging on sealed, smoked seafood isn't damaged and that the use-by date hasn't expired. If buying loose, it shouldn't have an unpleasant smell or dry edges. If salt cod is still flexible when you buy, wrap it in a damp towel and chill for up to three weeks; if it is rigid, wrap in foil and chill for up to three months. Always check the best-before dates on canned seafood.

Safe storage

Get your purchase home and refrigerated as soon as possible, ideally transporting it in an insulated bag. Remove all packaging and clean the fish with a damp cloth, then wrap it in wet kitchen paper and place on a lipped plate at the bottom of the fridge, at a temperature no higher than 4°C/40°F.

Leave live clams, mussels and oysters in their bag or put them in a dry bowl and cover with wet kitchen paper. Do not put them in a bowl of water or a sealed container, as they will die. Store oysters in their shells, rounded cup down, to keep them fresh in their juices, covered with a wet cloth or seaweed.

All shellfish should be stored in the bottom of the fridge and cooked or eaten within 12 hours. Fresh fish should also be cooked and eaten on the day of purchase, although most remain edible for another day if properly refrigerated. Oily fish spoils more quickly than white fish.

Refrigerate smoked or marinated seafood as soon as you get it home, and consume within two or three days, or by the use-by date.

WAYS TO COOK FISH

The Canadian Cooking Theory, developed some decades ago, advocates cooking fish for 10 minutes per 2.5 cm/1 inch at the thickest part for dry-heat methods. This is an easy approach for anyone new to seafood cooking, but many chefs today prefer 8–9 minutes for slightly less well-cooked fish. This is a matter of personal taste, so experiment and know how to tell when fish is cooked as you enjoy it: perfectly cooked fish is opaque with milky white juices and flakes and comes away from the bone easily; undercooked fish resists flaking, is translucent and has clear juices; overcooked fish looks dry and falls apart into thin pieces. Tuna and other meaty fish can be roasted and pan-seared like beef to be served rare, medium and well-done.

When you are chargrilling, sautéing and pan- and stir-frying, start with a well-heated pan or wok, so that the fish develops a crust that retains internal moisture.

Dry-heat cooking – barbecuing, grilling, chargrilling and roasting

Whole fish, fillets, steaks and kebabs can be cooked by these methods, and oily fish are particularly suited to grilling, barbecuing and chargrilling, because the natural oils they contain baste the flesh. Their full flavours are not overpowered by smoky aromas. Marinate white fish before barbecuing.

Barbecuing and grilling are similar, with the former cooking from the bottom and the latter from the top. In both cases, position the rack about 10 cm/4 inches from the heat. Brush the rack with oil, add the fish and cook until the flesh flakes

Unlike meat, fish have naturally tender flesh, so they need very little preparation and cooking. Fish can be cooked in several different ways, but the one thing to guard against is overcooking.

easily, basting with a marinade or melted butter. Ideally cook the fish without turning; if the surface is browning too quickly, adjust the rack position. Barbecue thin fillets and small fish, such as sardines, in a hinged fish basket.

Chargrilling is a quick way to give fish a barbecue flavour without having to light a barbecue. Heat a cast-iron griddle pan over a high heat, brush the fish with oil andchargrill until seared on one side and cooked through.

Whole fish are particularly delicious when roasted, as the skin and bones preserve the natural flavours. Preheat the oven to 230°C/450°F/Gas Mark 8 and make a few slashes on each side. Rub the fish with oil, put in a roasting pan and roast, uncovered, until the flesh comes away from the bone when tested – the skin becomes crisp, while the flesh remains tenderly moist.

Wet-heat cooking – poaching, steaming and stewing

Fish is excellent poached or steamed. Although these techniques are very easy, they can still overcook fish so pay close attention. Another advantage is that the cooking liquid can be incorporated into a tasty sauce to serve alongside. Poach in gently simmering liquid

CHARGRILLING

ROASTING

flavoured with lemon and herbs for 8–12 minutes per 2.5 cm/1 inch of thickness. When steaming, make sure the seasoned fish never actually touches the water. Steam, covered, for 3–5 minutes for fillets and steaks and 8–9 minutes per 2.5 cm/1 inch of thickness for whole fish.

Seafish stews often contain a variety of fish, simmered with other ingredients. To prevent overcooking, add the seafood towards the end, adding the most delicate pieces last – they will take only 2 or 3 minutes. Don't allow the liquid to boil.

Cooking in oil – sautéing, stir-frying and pan- and deep-frying

Fish steaks and fillets are most suited to these quick techniques. For sautéing and pan-frying, heat 5 mm/^{1}/4 inch vegetable oil in a hot sauté or frying pan, dust the fish with seasoned flour and fry over medium-high heat for 2–3 minutes on each side for thin fillets, and up to 5–6 minutes per side for steaks 2.5 cm/ 1 inch thick.

Successful deep-frying requires fish to be coated in batter or crumbs and for the oil to be maintained at a steady 180°C/350°F. If you don't have a deep-fat fryer with a controlled thermostat, use a heavy-based pan and a thermometer: if the temperature is too cool, the fried fish will be soggy; if it is too high, the outside will be overcooked while the centre will be raw. Work in batches to prevent overcrowding and a reduction in the oil's temperature.

DON'T FIDDLE WHEN SEARING, CHARGRILLING, GRILLING AND BARBECUING, AND DON'T BE TEMPTED TO TURN OR MOVE THE FISH AROUND WHILE COOKING, AS IT MAY STICK TO THE PAN OR RACK AND FALL APART. IDEALLY, TURN THE FISH ONLY ONCE DURING COOKING.

POACHING

BARBECUING   **PAN-FRYING**

BASIC RECIPES

The recipes in this book provide an unlimited variety of delicious fish meals. Some of the recipes use common basic recipes which are referred to on these pages, or you could use these basic recipes as an addition to a dish of your choice.

FISH STOCK

MAKES ABOUT 1.4 LITRES/2½ PINTS

- 900 G–1.3 KG/2–3 LB FISH HEADS, BONES AND TAILS, WITH ANY LARGE BONES CRACKED AND WITHOUT ANY GILLS
- 1.2 LITRES/2 PINTS WATER
- 500 ML/18 FL OZ DRY WHITE WINE
- 1 ONION, THINLY SLICED
- 1 LEEK, HALVED, RINSED AND CHOPPED
- 1 CARROT, PEELED AND SLICED
- 6 FRESH FLAT-LEAF PARSLEY SPRIGS
- 1 BAY LEAF
- 4 BLACK PEPPERCORNS, LIGHTLY CRUSHED

Put the fish trimmings, water and wine in a large, heavy-based saucepan over a medium–high heat and slowly bring to the boil, skimming the surface constantly to remove the grey foam.

When the foam stops forming, reduce the heat to low, add the remaining ingredients and leave the stock to simmer for 30 minutes, skimming the surface occasionally if necessary. Strain the stock and discard the flavouring ingredients. The stock is now ready to use or can be left to cool completely, then chilled for 1 day, as long as it is brought to a full rolling boil before use. Alternatively, it can be frozen for up to 6 months.

COURT BOUILLON

MAKES ABOUT 0.6 LITRES/1 PINT

- 850 ML/1½ PINTS COLD WATER
- 850 ML/1½ PINTS DRY WHITE WINE
- 3 TBSP WHITE WINE VINEGAR
- 2 LARGE CARROTS, ROUGHLY CHOPPED
- 1 ONION, ROUGHLY CHOPPED
- 2 CELERY STICKS, ROUGHLY CHOPPED
- 2 LEEKS, ROUGHLY CHOPPED
- 2 GARLIC CLOVES, ROUGHLY CHOPPED
- 2 FRESH BAY LEAVES
- 4 FRESH PARSLEY SPRIGS
- 6 BLACK PEPPERCORNS
- 1 TSP SEA SALT

Put all the ingredients into a large saucepan and slowly bring to the boil. Cover and simmer gently for 30 minutes. Strain the liquid through a fine sieve into a clean saucepan. Bring to the boil again and simmer fast, uncovered, for 15–20 minutes, until reduced to 600 ml/1 pint.

Simmer the fish in the court bouillon, according to the length of time required to cook. Drain the fish.

BÉCHAMEL SAUCE

- 300 ML/10 FL OZ MILK
- 4 CLOVES
- 1 BAY LEAF
- PINCH OF FRESHLY GRATED NUTMEG
- 25 G/1 OZ BUTTER OR MARGARINE
- 2 TBSP PLAIN FLOUR
- SALT AND PEPPER

Put the milk in a saucepan and add the cloves, bay leaf and nutmeg. Gradually bring to the boil. Remove from the heat and set aside for 15 minutes.
Melt the butter in another saucepan and stir in the flour to make a roux. Cook gently, stirring, for 1 minute. Remove the pan from the heat.
Strain the milk and gradually blend into the roux. Return the pan to the heat and gently bring to the boil, stirring, until the sauce thickens. Season to taste.

VARIATIONS

All sorts of ingredients can be added to the basic Béchamel recipe to make interesting sauces that go particularly well with vegetables and fish.

WATERCRESS SAUCE

Add a small bunch of watercress, finely chopped, to the basic sauce.

PARSLEY SAUCE

Add 2 tablespoons of finely chopped fresh parsley to the basic sauce.

MUSHROOM SAUCE

Add 115 g/4 oz finely sliced button mushrooms to the basic sauce with 1 tablespoon of finely chopped fresh tarragon.

LEMON SAUCE

Add some finely grated lemon rind and 1 teaspoon of lemon juice to the basic sauce.

MUSTARD SAUCE

Add 1 tablespoon of French mustard and a squeeze of lemon juice to the basic sauce.

HOLLANDAISE SAUCE

- 2 TBSP WHITE WINE VINEGAR
- 2 TBSP WATER
- 6 BLACK PEPPERCORNS
- 3 EGG YOLKS
- 250 G/9 OZ UNSALTED BUTTER
- 2 TSP LEMON JUICE
- SALT AND PEPPER

Put the wine vinegar and water into a small saucepan with the peppercorns, bring to the boil, then reduce the heat and simmer until it is reduced to 1 tablespoon (take care, as this happens very quickly). Strain.
Mix the egg yolks in a blender or food processor and add the strained vinegar while the machine is running.
Melt the butter in a small saucepan and heat until it is almost brown. While the blender is running, add three-quarters of the butter and the lemon juice, then add the remaining butter and season well with salt and pepper.
Turn the sauce into a serving bowl or keep warm for up to 1 hour in a bowl over a saucepan of warm water. If serving cold, allow to cool and store in the refrigerator for up to 2 days.

MAYONNAISE

- 2 EGG YOLKS
- 150 ML/5 FL OZ SUNFLOWER OIL
- 150 ML/5 FL OZ OLIVE OIL
- 1 TBSP WHITE WINE VINEGAR
- 2 TSP DIJON MUSTARD
- SALT AND PEPPER

Beat the egg yolks with a pinch of salt. Combine the oils in a jug. Gradually add one quarter of the oil mixture to the beaten egg, a drop at a time, beating constantly with a whisk or electric mixer.
Beat in the vinegar, then continue adding the combined oils in a steady stream, beating constantly.
Stir in the mustard and season to taste with salt and pepper.

AÏOLI

- 1 LARGE EGG YOLK
- 1 TBSP WHITE WINE VINEGAR OR LEMON JUICE
- 2 LARGE GARLIC CLOVES, PEELED AND CRUSHED
- 5 TBSP EXTRA VIRGIN OLIVE OIL
- 5 TBSP SUNFLOWER OIL
- SALT AND PEPPER

Put the egg yolk, vinegar, garlic, and salt and pepper to taste in a bowl and whisk until all the ingredients are well blended.
Add the olive oil, then the sunflower oil, drop by drop at first, and then, when the sauce begins to thicken, in a slow, steady stream until it is thick and smooth.

GREEK GARLIC SAUCE

- 115 G/4 OZ WHOLE BLANCHED ALMONDS
- 3 TBSP FRESH WHITE BREADCRUMBS
- 2 LARGE GARLIC CLOVES, CRUSHED
- 2 TSP LEMON JUICE
- 150 ML/5 FL OZ EXTRA VIRGIN OLIVE OIL
- 4 TBSP HOT WATER
- SALT AND PEPPER

Put the almonds in a food processor and blend until finely ground. Add the breadcrumbs, garlic, lemon juice, and salt and pepper to taste, and mix well together.
With the machine running, very slowly pour in the oil to form a smooth, thick mixture. When all the oil has been added, blend in the water.
Turn the mixture into a bowl and chill in the refrigerator for at least 2 hours before serving.

TARTARE SAUCE

- 2 LARGE EGG YOLKS
- 2 TSP DIJON MUSTARD
- 2 TBSP LEMON JUICE OR WHITE WINE VINEGAR
- ABOUT 300 ML/10 FL OZ SUNFLOWER OIL
- 10 CORNICHONS, FINELY CHOPPED
- 1 TBSP CAPERS, FINELY CHOPPED
- 1 TBSP FLAT-LEAF PARSLEY, FINELY CHOPPED
- SALT
- WHITE PEPPER

Whiz the egg yolks with the Dijon mustard, and salt and pepper to taste, in a food processor or blender or by hand. Add the lemon juice and whiz again.
With the motor still running or still beating, add the oil, drop by drop at first. When the sauce begins to thicken, the oil can then be added in a slow, steady stream.
Stir in the cornichons, capers and parsley. Taste and adjust the seasoning with extra salt, pepper and lemon juice if necessary. If the sauce seems too thick, slowly add 1 tablespoon of hot water.
Use at once or store in an airtight container in the refrigerator for up to 1 week.

SUSHI RICE

MAKES 1 QUANTITY

- 250 G/9 OZ SUSHI RICE
- 325 ML/11 FL OZ WATER
- 1 PIECE OF KOMBU
- 2 TBSP SUSHI RICE SEASONING

Wash the sushi rice under cold running water until the water running through it is clear, then drain the rice. Put the rice in a saucepan with the water and the kombu, then cover and bring to the boil as quickly as you can. Remove the kombu, then reduce the heat and simmer for 10 minutes. Turn off the heat and leave the rice to stand for 15 minutes. Do not take the lid off the saucepan once you have removed the kombu.

Put the hot rice in a large, very shallow bowl and pour the sushi rice seasoning evenly over the surface of the rice. Use one hand to mix the seasoning carefully into the rice with quick cutting strokes using a spatula, and the other to fan the sushi rice in order to cool it quickly.

The sushi rice should look shiny and be at room temperature when you are ready to use it.

BEURRE BLANC

- 3 TBSP VERY FINELY CHOPPED SHALLOTS
- 2 BAY LEAVES
- 6 BLACK PEPPERCORNS, LIGHTLY CRUSHED
- 3 TBSP WHITE WINE, SUCH AS MUSCADET
- 3 TBSP WHITE WINE VINEGAR
- 1$^{1}/_{2}$ TBSP DOUBLE CREAM
- 175 G/6 OZ UNSALTED BUTTER, CUT INTO SMALL PIECES
- 2 TSP CHOPPED FRESH TARRAGON
- SALT AND PEPPER

Put the shallots, bay leaves, peppercorns, wine and vinegar in a small saucepan over a medium–high heat and boil until reduced to about 1 tablespoon. Strain the mixture through a non-metallic sieve, then return the liquid to the saucepan. Stir the cream into the liquid and bring to the boil, then reduce the heat to low. Whisk in the butter, piece by piece, not adding the next until the previous one has melted. Whisking constantly and lifting the pan off the heat occasionally will help to prevent the sauce separating. Stir in the tarragon, and salt and pepper to taste, and serve immediately.

FLAT SEAFISH

Often regarded as the 'king of the seas', because of their fine texture and delicately-flavoured flesh, the fish in this chapter are very low in fat and high in protein. The thin fillets respond well to quick cooking techniques, such as pan-frying, which makes them perfect for quick meals. Another advantage of flat fish is that they are interchangeable in most recipes so if, for example, sole is too expensive, try plaice, flounder or halibut.

THE FLAT SEAFISH DIRECTORY

The following is a guide to all the main species of flat fish that can be eaten, listed by their common names, although some fish, confusingly, are known by a variety of different names. The potted profile for each fish details the various forms in which it can be purchased, for example whole or in fillets, fresh or canned, and the most suitable cooking methods.

PLAICE

One of the most popular flat fish, it is distinguished by the large red or orange spots on its brown back. It is available whole or in fillets and its white flesh can be fried, grilled, poached, steamed or baked.

FLOUNDER

Flounder is very similar to plaice, but its flavour and texture are not so fine. It is available whole or in fillets and can be cooked in the same way as plaice. In the US, flounder is a collective name for several varieties of flat fish.

TURBOT

This fish, with its huge brown, knobbly body and small head, is considered the finest of the flat fish. It is low in fat, has firm, snow-white flesh and a fine, delicate taste. Depending on its size, it is available whole, in cutlets or in fillets and can be baked, poached or steamed.

BRILL

Brill is smaller but not dissimilar to turbot in flavour and texture. It is usually sold whole, but can be halved, sliced or filleted and lends itself to being cooked by any method.

SKATE & RAY

This strange-looking fish is shaped like a kite. There are several varieties, of which only the fish's pectoral fins, known as its wings, and small pieces of flesh cut from the bony part of the fish, known as nobs, are eaten. It is low in fat and has a superior flavour. The common skate is particularly vulnerable to overfishing and is listed as endangered (see the best choices to make in the Marine Conservation Society Good Fish Guide on page 16–17).

DOVER SOLE

This is one of the finest-flavoured and finest-textured small flat fish. Its white flesh has an exquisite flavour. Available whole or in fillets, it is traditionally grilled or fried, a classic recipe being Sole Meunière.

HALIBUT

This large flat fish is available whole or as cutlets or fillets. Its flesh is quite oily and its firm texture makes it suitable for a variety of cooking methods, including baking, braising, poaching or steaming. Halibut is vulnerable to overfishing (see the best choices to make in the Marine Conservation Society Good Fish Guide on page 16–17).

LEMON SOLE

Lemon sole is not dissimilar to Dover sole, although it has far less flavour, and while its white flesh has a fine texture it is less firm. It can be purchased and cooked in the same way as Dover sole.

DAB

This is one of the smallest flat fish and belongs to the plaice family. It has a rough, light brown upper skin and white flesh. It is available whole or in fillets and can be cooked in the same way as plaice.

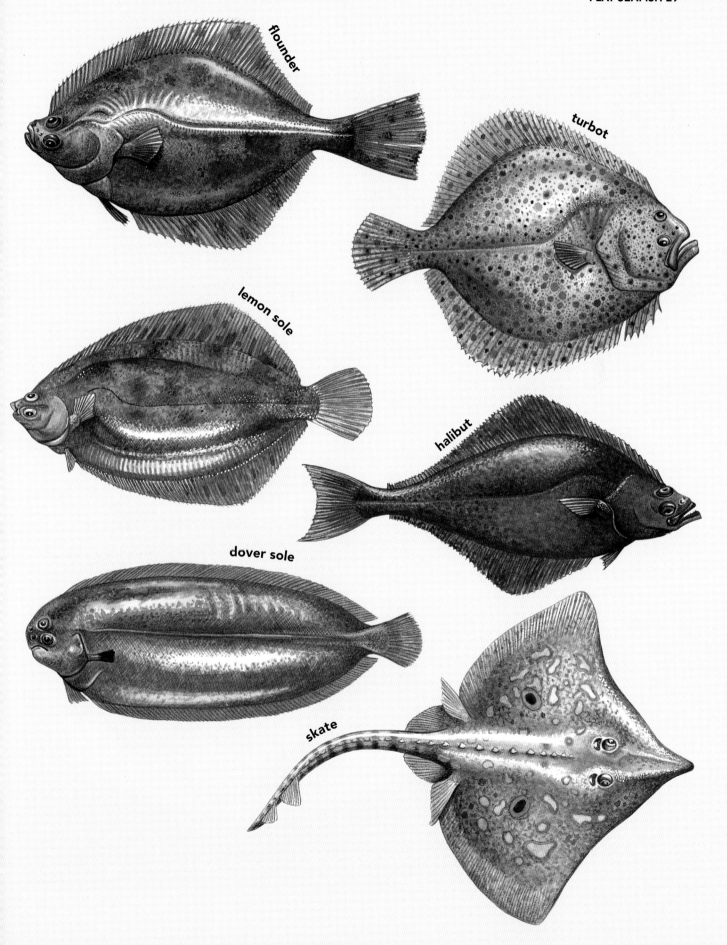

flounder

turbot

lemon sole

halibut

dover sole

skate

GUTTING AND TRIMMING A FLAT SEAFISH

Before preparing fish it must be cleaned. This involves removing the entrails and gills and sometimes the scales and fins. Your fish supplier should do this for you – if not, the following guidelines provide a step-by-step method.

Trimming a flat seafish

If desired, using kitchen scissors, cut off the gills and fins if the fish is to be served whole. The head and tail may also be cut off using a sharp knife. Rinse the cavity under cold running water. Fins and scales obviously don't need to be removed if the fish is to be filleted or the skin is to be removed after cooking.

Gutting a flat seafish

The entrails of a flat fish occupy only a small part of the fish's body cavity. To remove them, open the cavity, which lies in the upper part of the body under the gills, pull out the entrails and clean away any blood in the cavity.

FLOUNDER FOR TWO (SEE PAGE 52)

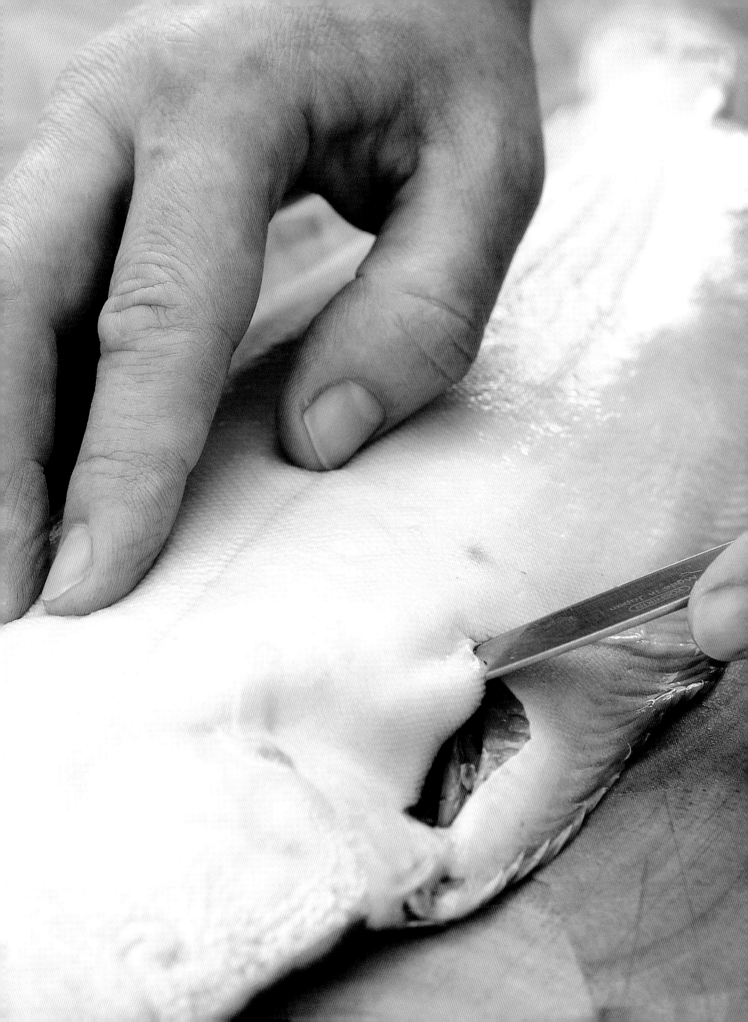

FILLETING AND SKINNING A FLAT SEAFISH

A very sharp knife will be required for this task, as the skin of flat fish, especially that of flounder, is quite tough.

Filleting a flat seafish

Four fillets, two from each side, are usually taken from a flat fish, although sometimes one large fillet is cut from each side – these are known as double or butterfly fillets. To make four fillets, put the fish on a chopping board with its tail towards you. Using a sharp knife, cut around the shape of the head and along the backbone from head to tail. With smooth cutting strokes, working from head to tail, separate the flesh from the bone. Turn the fish over and repeat on the other side.

Skinning whole flat seafish

Whole flat fish are usually cooked with the skin on. However, Dover and slip soles are traditionally skinned on the dark side only before cooking.

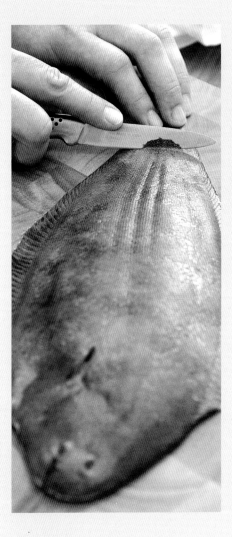

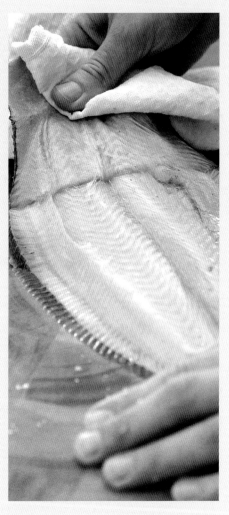

1 Using a sharp knife, make a small cut in the dark skin across the tail.

2 Slip your thumb between the skin and flesh of the fish and loosen the skin. Then, holding the tail end firmly with one hand and gripping the skin with a cloth or kitchen paper in the other hand, pull the skin upwards towards the head. A large pinch of salt may help you to grip the flesh.

BONING A DOVER OR SLIP SOLE

Dover and slip soles can be boned in preparation for stuffing. To do this, first skin both sides of the fish as described opposite under Filleting and Skinning a Flat Seafish.

1 Put the fish on a chopping board with its tail towards you and, using a sharp knife, cut around the shape of the head and along the backbone from head to tail.

2 With smooth cutting strokes, working from head to tail, lift the flesh from the bone, stopping when you reach the fins. Leave the fillet completely attached to the fins, head and tail. Turn the fish around and separate the fillet on the other side of the fish in the same way.

3 Turn the fish over and repeat on the other side, leaving the fillets attached to the fins, head and tail in the same way. Using kitchen scissors, cut away all around the backbone and remove it.

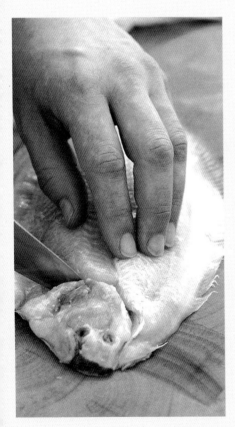

PAN-FRIED HALIBUT STEAKS WITH TOMATO SALSA

SERVES 4

INGREDIENTS

- 4 HALIBUT STEAKS, EACH ABOUT 2.5 CM/1 INCH THICK
- 1 TBSP VEGETABLE OIL
- 50 G/1¾ OZ BUTTER
- FLOUR, FOR DUSTING
- JUICE OF ½ LEMON
- SALT AND PEPPER

TOMATO SALSA

- 3 FIRM TOMATOES, HALVED, DESEEDED AND FINELY DICED
- 1 SMALL RED ONION, FINELY DICED
- 1 FRESH GREEN CHILLI, DESEEDED AND FINELY CHOPPED
- 3 TBSP CHOPPED FRESH CORIANDER
- JUICE OF 1 LIME
- ½ TSP SEA SALT

1 Rinse the fish under cold running water and pat dry with kitchen paper.

2 Combine all the salsa ingredients in a serving bowl and leave to stand at room temperature.

3 Heat the oil and 40 g/1½ oz of the butter in a large frying pan over a medium–high heat. Dust the halibut steaks with flour and season to taste with salt and pepper. Place in the pan and cook for 5 minutes on one side, then turn over and cook for 3–4 minutes on the other side, until golden and cooked through. Transfer to a warmed serving dish.

4 Add the lemon juice to the pan and simmer over a medium heat for a few seconds, scraping up any sediment from the base of the pan. Stir in the remaining butter and cook for a few seconds. Pour over the fish and serve immediately with the salsa.

PLAICE ROASTED WITH LIME

SERVES 4

INGREDIENTS

- 4 PLAICE FILLETS, EACH ABOUT 250 G/9 OZ
- JUICE OF 1 LIME
- 3 TBSP EXTRA VIRGIN OLIVE OIL
- 1 LARGE ONION, FINELY CHOPPED
- 3 GARLIC CLOVES, FINELY CHOPPED
- 2–3 PICKLED JALAPEÑO CHILLIES (JALAPEÑOS EN ESCABECHE), CHOPPED
- 6–8 TBSP CHOPPED FRESH CORIANDER, PLUS EXTRA SPRIGS TO GARNISH
- SALT AND PEPPER
- LIME WEDGES, TO SERVE

1 Preheat the oven to 180°C/350°F/Gas Mark 4.

2 Rinse the fish under cold running water and pat dry with kitchen paper. Place the fish fillets in a non-metallic bowl and season to taste with salt and pepper. Sprinkle the lime juice over the fish.

3 Heat the oil in a frying pan. Add the onion and garlic and cook, stirring frequently, for 2 minutes, or until softened. Remove the frying pan from the heat.

4 Place a third of the onion mixture and a little of the chillies and chopped coriander in the base of a shallow ovenproof dish or roasting tin. Arrange the fish on top. Top with the remaining onion mixture, chillies and chopped coriander.

5 Roast in the preheated oven for 15–20 minutes, or until the fish has become slightly opaque and firm to the touch. Garnish with coriander sprigs and serve immediately with lime wedges for squeezing over.

PLAICE WITH A FLUFFY CHEESE TOPPING

SERVES 4

INGREDIENTS

- 55 G/2 OZ UNSALTED BUTTER, PLUS EXTRA FOR GREASING
- 900 G/2 LB PLAICE FILLETS
- 1 RED PEPPER, DESEEDED AND THINLY SLICED
- 600 ML/1 PINT MAYONNAISE
- 225 G/8 OZ CHEDDAR CHEESE, GRATED
- 4 TBSP DOUBLE CREAM
- 4 EGG WHITES
- SALT AND PEPPER
- SPRIGS OF FRESH WATERCRESS, TO GARNISH

1 Preheat the oven to 180°C/350°F/Gas Mark 4. Grease a large ovenproof dish with butter.

2 Melt the butter in a large, heavy-based frying pan. Add the fish fillets, in batches, and cook over a medium heat for 2 minutes on each side. Using a fish slice, transfer the fish to a chopping board and carefully remove and discard the skin, then put the fillets in the prepared dish. Sprinkle the red pepper slices on top.

3 Mix together the mayonnaise, cheese and cream in a bowl and season to taste with salt and pepper. Whisk the egg whites in a grease-free bowl until stiff but not dry. Gently fold the egg whites into the mayonnaise mixture.

4 Pour the mayonnaise mixture over the fish to cover it completely. Place the dish on a baking tray and bake for 20 minutes, until the topping is fluffy and lightly browned. Serve immediately, garnished with the watercress.

HALIBUT WITH CARAMELIZED ONIONS

SERVES 1

INGREDIENTS

- 1 TBSP VEGETABLE OIL
- ½ SMALL ONION, THINLY SLICED
- ½ TSP BALSAMIC VINEGAR
- 1 TBSP BUTTER, MELTED
- 115 G/4 OZ HALIBUT FILLET OR HALIBUT STEAK
- SPRIGS OF FRESH FLAT-LEAF PARSLEY, TO GARNISH
- NEW POTATOES AND TOMATO QUARTERS, TO SERVE

1 Heat the oil in a large frying pan over a medium heat. Add the onion, stir well and reduce the heat. Cook for 15–20 minutes over a very low heat, stirring occasionally, until the onion is very soft and brown.

2 Add the vinegar to the pan and cook for 2 minutes, stirring constantly to prevent sticking.

3 Brush the melted butter over the fish.

4 Preheat the grill to hot. Sear the fish, then reduce the heat and cook for about 10 minutes, turning once. The cooking time will depend on the thickness of the fillet, but the fish should be firm and tender when done.

5 Remove the fish from the heat, place on a serving platter and top with the caramelized onion. Garnish with the parsley and serve with the potatoes and tomatoes.

SOLE MEUNIÈRE

SERVES 2

INGREDIENTS

- ABOUT 100 ML/3½ FL OZ MILK
- 4 TBSP PLAIN FLOUR
- 4 SOLE FILLETS, ABOUT 175 G/6 OZ EACH, ALL DARK SKIN AND BONES REMOVED
- 85 G/3 OZ BUTTER
- JUICE OF ½ LEMON
- SALT AND PEPPER
- CHOPPED FRESH FLAT-LEAF PARSLEY, TO GARNISH
- COOKED ASPARAGUS AND LEMON WEDGES, TO SERVE

1 Pour the milk into a flat dish at least as large as the fillets and put the flour on a plate. Season each fillet on both sides with salt and pepper to taste.

2 Working with 1 fillet at a time, pull it very quickly through the milk, then put it in the flour, turn once to coat all over and shake off the excess flour. Continue until all the fillets are prepared.

3 Melt half the butter in a sauté pan or frying pan large enough to hold the fillets in a single layer over a medium–high heat. Add the fillets to the pan, skinned side down, and fry for 2 minutes.

4 Turn over the fillets and fry for 2–3 minutes, or until the flesh flakes easily. Transfer to warmed serving plates, skinned side up, and reserve.

5 Reduce the heat to medium and melt the remaining butter in the pan. When it stops foaming, add the lemon juice and stir, scraping the sediment from the base of the pan. Spoon the butter over the fish and sprinkle with the parsley. Serve with the asparagus and lemon wedges.

SOLE GOUJONS WITH TARTARE SAUCE

SERVES 4

INGREDIENTS

- 8 SOLE FILLETS, ABOUT 85 G/3 OZ EACH, ALL SKIN AND BONES REMOVED
- 3–4 TBSP PLAIN FLOUR
- 85 G/3 OZ FINE FRESH WHITE BREADCRUMBS
- 2 LARGE EGGS
- SUNFLOWER OIL, FOR DEEP-FRYING
- SALT AND PEPPER
- TARTARE SAUCE (SEE PAGE 24) AND LEMON WEDGES, TO SERVE

1 Preheat the oven to its lowest temperature. Cut the sole fillets into strips about 7.5 cm/3 inches long and 1 cm/½ inch wide, then set aside.

2 Put the flour with salt and pepper to taste in a polythene bag. Put the breadcrumbs on a flat plate and lightly beat the eggs with salt and pepper to taste in a large flat bowl, such as a soup plate.

3 Heat enough oil for deep-frying in a heavy-based saucepan to 180–190°C/350–375°F, or until a cube of bread browns in 30 seconds. Toss about a quarter of the fish strips in the seasoned flour, then shake off any excess flour. Quickly dip the fish strips in the egg, then coat with the breadcrumbs, making sure the fish is completely covered.

4 Drop the goujons into the hot oil and deep-fry for 2–3 minutes until golden and crisp. Use a slotted spoon to scoop out the goujons and drain them well on crumpled kitchen paper. Sprinkle with extra salt and keep warm in the oven while frying the remaining goujons, returning the oil to the correct temperature, if necessary, before frying each batch.

5 Continue until all the fish is fried. Serve with the Tartare Sauce on the side and lemon wedges for squeezing.

NORMANDY SOLE

SERVES 4

INGREDIENTS
- 350 G/12 OZ LIVE MUSSELS
- 300 ML/10 FL OZ DRY WHITE WINE
- 1 BOUQUET GARNI
- 225 G/8 OZ UNPEELED COOKED PRAWNS
- 2 SHALLOTS, CHOPPED
- 8 LEMON SOLE FILLETS, EACH ABOUT 85 G/3 OZ, SKINNED
- 85 G/3 OZ UNSALTED BUTTER
- 115 G/4 OZ BUTTON MUSHROOMS, THINLY SLICED
- 40 G/1½ OZ PLAIN FLOUR
- 300 ML/10 FL OZ DOUBLE CREAM
- SALT AND PEPPER
- CHOPPED FRESH PARSLEY, TO GARNISH
- COOKED MANGETOUT, TO SERVE

1 Scrub the mussels under cold running water and pull off the 'beards'. Discard any mussels with broken shells or that do not shut when sharply tapped. Put them in a large saucepan, pour in the wine, add the bouquet garni and season with salt and pepper.

2 Cover the pan with a tight-fitting lid and bring to the boil. Cook, shaking the pan occasionally, for 3–5 minutes, until the shells have opened. Drain the mussels, reserving the cooking liquid, and discard any that have remained closed. Remove the mussels from their shells and set them aside. Discard the bouquet garni.

3 Strain the reserved cooking liquid through a muslin-lined sieve into a clean saucepan. Peel the prawns and set aside. Add the shells to the pan with the shallots. Bring to the boil over a medium heat, then reduce the heat, cover and simmer gently for 15 minutes.

4 Strain the prawn stock and return it to the saucepan. Add the fish fillets – they usually fit better if folded in half. Bring just to the boil, then reduce the heat, cover and poach very gently for 5–8 minutes, until the flesh flakes easily.

5 Meanwhile, melt half the butter in a frying pan. Add the mushrooms and cook over a low heat, stirring occasionally, for 5 minutes, until tender.

6 Using a fish slice, drain the fish, and carefully transfer to a warmed serving dish and keep warm. Strain and reserve the prawn stock.

7 Melt the remaining butter in a saucepan over a low heat. Stir in the flour and cook, stirring constantly, for 2 minutes. Remove the pan from the heat and gradually stir in the cream, then the prawn stock. Return the pan to the heat and bring to the boil, stirring constantly. Reduce the heat and cook, stirring, for 2–3 minutes, until thickened and smooth. Season to taste with salt and pepper and stir in the mussels, prawns and mushrooms. Heat through gently for 2–3 minutes, then spoon the sauce over the fish. Sprinkle with the chopped parsley and serve immediately with the mangetout.

FISHERMAN'S PIE

SERVES 6

INGREDIENTS

- 900 G/2 LB WHITE FISH FILLETS, SUCH AS PLAICE, SKINNED
- 150 ML/5 FL OZ DRY WHITE WINE
- 1 TBSP CHOPPED FRESH PARSLEY, TARRAGON OR DILL
- 100 G/3½ OZ BUTTER, PLUS EXTRA FOR GREASING
- 175 G/6 OZ SMALL MUSHROOMS, SLICED
- 175 G/6 OZ COOKED PEELED PRAWNS
- 40 G/1½ OZ PLAIN FLOUR
- 125 ML/4 FL OZ DOUBLE CREAM
- 900 G/2 LB FLOURY POTATOES, SUCH AS KING EDWARD, MARIS PIPER OR DESIRÉE, PEELED AND CUT INTO CHUNKS
- SALT AND PEPPER

1 Preheat the oven to 180°C/350°F/Gas Mark 4. Grease a 1.7-litre/3-pint baking dish.

2 Fold the fish fillets in half and put in the dish. Season well with salt and pepper, pour over the wine and scatter over the parsley.

3 Cover with foil and bake in the preheated oven for 15 minutes until the fish starts to flake. Strain off the liquid and reserve for the sauce. Increase the oven temperature to 220°C/425°F/Gas Mark 7.

4 Melt 15 g/½ oz of the butter in a frying pan over a medium heat, add the mushrooms and cook, stirring frequently, for 5 minutes. Spoon over the fish. Scatter over the prawns.

5 Heat 55 g/2 oz of the remaining butter in a saucepan and stir in the flour. Cook for 3–4 minutes without browning, stirring constantly. Remove from the heat and gradually add the reserved cooking liquid, stirring well after each addition.

6 Return to the heat and slowly bring to the boil, stirring constantly, until thickened. Add the cream and season to taste with salt and pepper. Pour over the fish in the dish and smooth over the surface.

7 Bring a large saucepan of lightly salted water to the boil, add the potatoes and cook for 15–20 minutes. Drain well and mash with a potato masher until smooth. Season to taste with salt and pepper and add the remaining butter, stirring until melted.

8 Pile or pipe the potato onto the fish and sauce and bake for 10–15 minutes until golden brown.

NUT-CRUSTED HALIBUT

SERVES 4

INGREDIENTS

- 3 TBSP BUTTER, MELTED
- 750 G/1 LB 10 OZ HALIBUT FILLET
- 55 G/2 OZ PISTACHIO NUTS, SHELLED AND VERY FINELY CHOPPED
- MIXED SALAD AND LEMON WEDGES, TO SERVE

1 Brush the melted butter over the halibut fillet.

2 Spread out the nuts on a large, flat plate. Roll the fish in the nuts, pressing down gently.

3 Preheat a griddle over a medium heat. Cook the halibut, turning once, for 10 minutes, or until firm but tender – the exact cooking time will depend on the thickness of the fillet.

4 Remove the fish and any loose pistachio pieces from the heat and transfer to a large, warmed serving platter. Serve immediately, accompanied by the mixed salad and lemon wedges.

FLOUNDER FOR TWO

SERVES 2

INGREDIENTS

- 150 ML/5 FL OZ OLIVE OIL
- 375 G/13 OZ WAXY POTATOES, PEELED AND THINLY SLICED
- 1 FENNEL BULB, THINLY SLICED
- 2 LARGE TOMATOES, GRILLED, PEELED, DESEEDED AND CHOPPED
- 2 SHALLOTS, SLICED
- 1–2 WHOLE FLOUNDERS, CLEANED, ABOUT 1.3 KG/3 LB
- 4 TBSP DRY WHITE WINE
- 2 TBSP FINELY CHOPPED FRESH PARSLEY
- SALT AND PEPPER
- LEMON WEDGES, TO SERVE

1 Preheat the oven to 200°C/400°F/Gas Mark 6. Spread 4 tablespoons of the oil over the base of a shallow roasting tin large enough to hold the flounder. Arrange the potatoes in a single layer, then top with the fennel, tomatoes and shallots. Season to taste with salt and pepper. Drizzle with a further 4 tablespoons of the oil. Roast the vegetables in the preheated oven for 30 minutes.

2 Season the fish to taste with salt and pepper and put on top of the vegetables. Sprinkle with the wine and the remaining oil.

3 Return the roasting tin to the oven and roast the fish, uncovered, for 20 minutes, or until the flesh flakes easily.

4 To serve, skin the fish and remove the fillets. Sprinkle the parsley over the vegetables. Arrange 2–4 fillets on each plate, with the vegetables spooned alongside, accompanied by the lemon wedges for squeezing over.

PLAICE WITH EGG & DILL SAUCE

SERVES 4

INGREDIENTS

- 85 G/3 OZ BUTTER, PLUS EXTRA FOR GREASING
- 4 PLAICE FILLETS, EACH ABOUT 225 G/8 OZ
- JUICE OF 1/2 LEMON
- 4 HARD-BOILED EGGS, FINELY CHOPPED
- 4 CORNICHONS OR OTHER SMALL GHERKINS, FINELY CHOPPED
- 2 TBSP CHOPPED FRESH DILL
- SALT AND PEPPER
- FRESH DILL SPRIGS, TO GARNISH

1 Preheat the grill to medium. Generously grease a baking sheet with butter and put the fish fillets on it, skin side down.

2 Melt the butter in a saucepan over a low heat. Remove the pan from the heat and brush some of the butter over the fish. Set the remainder aside. Season the fish with salt and pepper, place under the grill and cook for 8 minutes, without turning, until the flesh flakes easily.

3 Just before the fish is cooked, stir the lemon juice, eggs, cornichons and chopped dill into the remaining melted butter. Heat gently, stirring occasionally, for 2 minutes.

4 Using a fish slice, transfer the fish fillets to warmed serving plates. Spoon over the sauce, garnish with the dill sprigs and serve immediately.

LEMON SOLE WITH PINK PEPPERCORNS & APPLES

SERVES 4

INGREDIENTS

- 300 ML/10 FL OZ FISH STOCK (SEE PAGE 22)
- 8 LEMON SOLE FILLETS, EACH ABOUT 85 G/3 OZ, SKINNED
- 1 TBSP PINK PEPPERCORNS
- 6 TBSP CRÈME FRAÎCHE
- 3 TART GREEN EATING APPLES, CORED AND THINLY SLICED
- SALT
- SPRIGS OF FRESH FLAT-LEAF PARSLEY, TO GARNISH

1 Pour all but 3 tablespoons of the stock into a saucepan. Add the fish fillets – they usually fit better if folded in half. Bring just to the boil, then reduce the heat, cover and poach very gently for 5–8 minutes, until the flesh flakes easily.

2 Meanwhile, put the peppercorns into another saucepan with the remaining fish stock and bring to the boil over a low heat. Stir in the crème fraîche, season with salt and cook, stirring frequently, for 3–5 minutes, until reduced. Add the apples and cook for 1–2 minutes, until soft but still firm.

3 Using a fish slice, drain the fish and transfer carefully to a warmed serving plate. Using a slotted spoon, transfer the apple slices to the plate to surround the fish. Keep warm.

4 Bring the peppercorn mixture back to the boil and gradually stir in enough of the fish cooking liquid to make a sauce. Spoon the sauce over the fish and serve immediately, garnished with the parsley sprigs.

FILLETS OF SOLE IN TOMATO & OLIVE SAUCE

SERVES 4

INGREDIENTS

- 4 TBSP OLIVE OIL
- 900 G/2 LB PLUM TOMATOES, PEELED, DESEEDED AND CHOPPED
- 2 TBSP SUN-DRIED TOMATO PURÉE
- 3 GARLIC CLOVES, FINELY CHOPPED
- 1 TBSP CHOPPED FRESH OREGANO
- 85 G/3 OZ PLAIN FLOUR
- 4 SOLE, FILLETED
- 85 G/3 OZ UNSALTED BUTTER
- 115 G/4 OZ BLACK OLIVES, STONED
- SALT AND PEPPER
- ROCKET LEAVES, TO SERVE

1 Heat the olive oil in a large, heavy-based saucepan. Add the tomatoes, tomato purée, garlic and oregano and season with salt and pepper. Stir well, then cover and simmer, stirring occasionally, for 30 minutes, until the mixture is thickened and pulpy.

2 Meanwhile, spread out the flour on a plate and season with salt and pepper. Coat the fish fillets in the seasoned flour, shaking off any excess.

3 Melt half the butter in a heavy-based frying pan. Add as many fillets as the frying pan will hold in a single layer and cook over a medium heat for 2 minutes on each side. Using a fish slice, transfer the fillets to an ovenproof dish and keep warm. Cook the remaining fillets, adding the remaining butter as required.

4 Stir the olives into the tomato sauce, then pour it over the fish. Bake in a preheated oven, 180°C/350°F/Gas Mark 4, for 20 minutes. Serve immediately, straight from the dish, accompanied by the rocket leaves.

GRILLED HALIBUT WITH GARLIC BUTTER

SERVES 4

INGREDIENTS

- 4 HALIBUT FILLETS, ABOUT 175 G/6 OZ EACH
- 6 TBSP BUTTER, PLUS EXTRA FOR GREASING
- 2 GARLIC CLOVES, FINELY CHOPPED
- SALT AND PEPPER
- SPRIGS OF FRESH FLAT-LEAF PARSLEY, TO GARNISH
- COOKED FRENCH BEANS AND LIME WEDGES, TO SERVE

1 Preheat the grill to medium. Rinse the fish fillets under cold running water, then pat dry with kitchen paper.

2 Grease a shallow, heatproof dish with butter, then arrange the fish in it. Season with salt and pepper.

3 In a separate bowl, mix the remaining butter with the garlic. Arrange pieces of the garlic butter all over the fish, then transfer to the grill. Cook for 7–8 minutes, turning once, until the fish is cooked through.

4 Remove the dish from the grill. Using a fish slice, remove the fillets from the dish and arrange on individual serving plates. Pour over the remaining melted butter from the dish, and garnish with the parsley sprigs. Serve with the French beans and lime wedges.

ROUND SEAFISH

This diverse fish family includes the oily fish mackerel, salmon and tuna, which, as well as being quick and easy to prepare, are also said to reduce the risk of stroke and heart disease when eaten regularly. Whereas most seafood is overpowered by full-flavoured herbs and spices, these fish soak up the flavours to make satisfying family meals. This is also where you'll find a fail-safe recipe for that great British classic, Fish & Chips.

THE ROUND SEAFISH DIRECTORY

The following is a guide to all the main species of round seafish that can be eaten, listed by their common names, although some fish, confusingly, are known by a variety of different names. The potted profile for each fish details the various forms in which it can be purchased, for example whole or in fillets, fresh or canned, and the most suitable cooking methods.

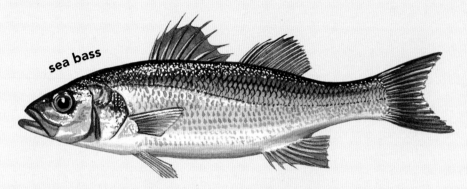

sea bass

SEA BASS/BASS

This large, sleek fish, similar in shape to the salmon, has dark, silver-grey scales, which should be removed before cooking, and a white belly. Its firm, white flesh has an excellent flavour. It can be bought whole or in cutlets or fillets and is suitable for poaching or steaming.

COD

This very popular, white-fleshed fish varies enormously in size and is available whole, which is particularly suitable for baking, poaching or steaming, and in fillets and cutlets, which can be fried or grilled. It is commonly used in cooked dishes such as Flaky Pastry Fish Pie. Much of it is frozen aboard fishing boats. It is also available salted, smoked and dried. Cod's roe is available fresh and smoked.

COLEY/SAITHE COALFISH

Coley is related to the cod family and has pinkish-grey flesh that becomes white when cooked. Usually available as fillets or cutlets, it can be used in the same way as cod but, as it can be dry, is not suitable for grilling. It is used in soups, stews and fish pies.

HOKI

Imported from New Zealand, hoki is related to hake, which, in turn, is a member of the cod family. Its white flesh is firm, contains very few bones and has a mild flavour. It is sold in fillets or pieces and can be baked, fried or grilled.

HADDOCK

This fish has a firm, white flesh and is closely related to cod, although it is usually smaller and can be distinguished by the dark streak that runs down its back and the two black marks either side of its gills. Sold as fillets or cutlets, it is interchangeable with cod in recipes and is used as an alternative when serving fish and chips. Haddock is often smoked – it is used as such in the well known dish Kedgeree.

MONKFISH/ ANGLER FISH

This deep sea fish has such a large, ugly head that usually only the tail is sold, boned as a whole piece or skinned and filleted. The monkfish is a species that matures late and is therefore vulnerable to overfishing (see the best choices to make in the Marine Conservation Society Good Fish Guide on page 16–17).

PARROT FISH

This beautiful tropical fish, with skin ranging in colour from turquoise and green to pink and violet, and its round, beak-like face really does look like a parrot. Its flesh is white and firm and is best cooked whole.

POMFRET

This silver, fairly small fish from warm waters is a round fish but, like the John Dory, is laterally compressed and therefore prepared as though a flat fish. It is similar to butterfish, which is popular in America. The flesh is white and delicate and can be stuffed and baked whole or filleted and fried or grilled.

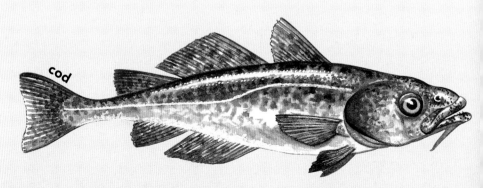

cod

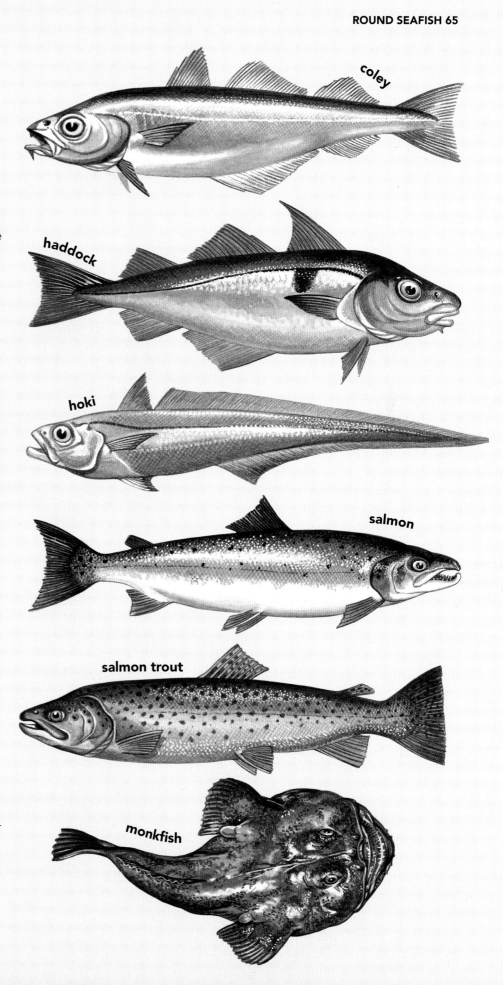

coley

haddock

hoki

salmon

salmon trout

monkfish

RED MULLET

Red mullet, of which there are several species, is unrelated to grey mullet. It looks attractive, with its crimson skin. It has a firm, white flesh, which has a delicate flavour. Its liver, too, is considered a delicacy, which is why it is usually sold uncleaned. For this reason, it should be eaten fresh before it deteriorates. It must be scaled before cooking and is usually cooked whole, fried, grilled or baked.

SALMON

Most salmon varieties mature at sea and then return to coastal rivers and streams to spawn. Atlantic salmon (wild salmon) and farmed salmon are available, and increased harvests of farmed salmon have made this popular fish more affordable. Salmon has a high fat content and a firm flesh, which can be pink to dark red. It can be poached or baked whole and its cutlets or fillets can be fried or grilled. Its red roe is available as salmon caviar, although this description really applies only to sturgeon roe. It is also popular canned and smoked. Smoked salmon is dry-salted before being smoked and is sold in fillets, which are cut into paper-thin slices.

SALMON TROUT/ SEA TROUT

This fish is often confused with salmon as it also returns from the sea to spawn in coastal rivers. It is smaller than salmon, but larger than trout, has pale pink flesh and can be used in the same way as salmon or trout. However, it is too delicate for smoking. It can be purchased whole or as fillets.

WHITING

This fish, related to hake, is fairly small and has pale brown skin and a cream belly. Its flesh is white and very soft, with a bland flavour. It can be bought fresh, either whole or in fillets, as well as smoked or salted. It is suitable for frying, grilling, poaching or steaming.

SEA BREAM

There are numerous varieties of this large fish, including the red, black, white, pink, ray and gilt-head sea bream. All have firm, white flesh, but the red bream is generally considered to have the best flavour. It is usually cooked whole and can be stuffed and baked, grilled or braised. Its interesting story is that they start life as males and later turn into females!

GREY MULLET

This fish, unrelated to the red mullet, looks and tastes similar to sea bass. It has firm, white flesh and can be bought whole or in fillets and is best baked or grilled.

BARRACUDA

This large, fierce fish from warm waters has white flesh with a firm texture. Small barracuda can be filleted and are suitable for baking, frying, grilling, poaching, steaming and for using in soups and stews. Never eat barracuda raw, or its liver, as it can be toxic.

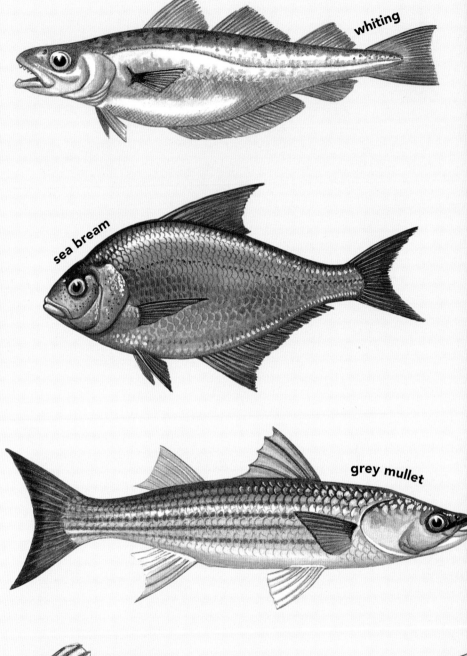

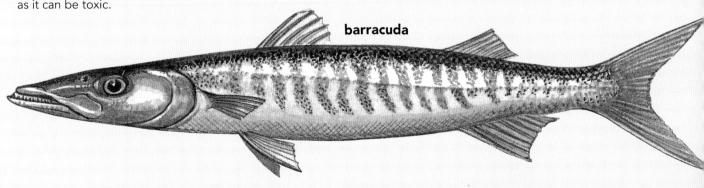

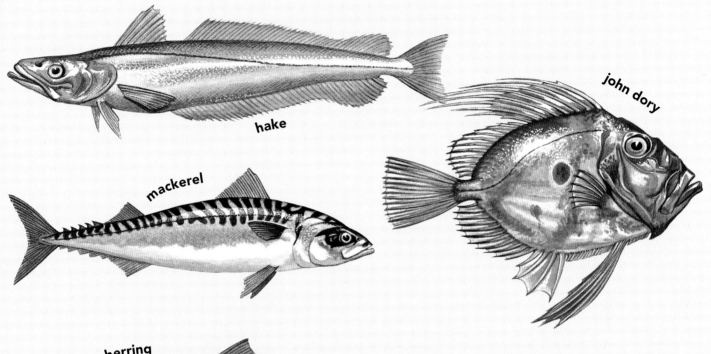

HAKE

This large fish is a member of the cod family, but has a slightly firmer, white flesh. Large hake are cut into fillets or cutlets and these are usually poached, but they can also be fried or grilled. Small hake are sold whole. Smoked hake is also available, as well as salted hake, which is prepared and used in the same way as salt cod.

HERRING

A small, very oily fish, available whole or filleted, that can be fried or grilled or stuffed and baked. Due to its oiliness, the herring is ideal for preserving. Rollmop herrings are raw herrings, boned, rolled up with chopped onions, gherkins and peppercorns and then marinated in spiced vinegar. Herrings are also smoked. Kippers are the most popular form and are sold in fillets or whole, often in pairs. Ideally, dye should not be used in the process. Buckling is another version of smoked herring, one that is often considered the best, and lightly salted bloaters and smoked herrings are also available. Herrings can be preserved between layers of salt. Canned herring is also popular.

JOHN DORY/DORY

In most parts of the world, John Dory is called St Peter or St Pierre (not to be confused with St Peter's Fish), but not in the UK, Greece or Portugal. Although strictly speaking a round fish, John Dory is laterally compressed and therefore prepared as a flat fish, from which there is little flesh and much waste. It has an ugly head with a very large jaw and a large mark on its side like a thumb print. When fresh it is golden in colour and its firm, white flesh has a delicate flavour. It is usually filleted and fried and it is also a traditional ingredient in the traditional Mediterranean fish stew bouillabaisse.

MACKEREL

This fish, with its striking black markings and silver belly, is particularly oily, which makes it ideal for frying and grilling or stuffing and baking. As its dark flesh has a distinctive flavour, it is often accompanied by a sharp-flavoured sauce, such as gooseberry. Mackerel is available whole or in fillets as well as canned or smoked. Smoked mackerel has a rich, strong flavour and is sold in fillets that are sometimes peppered or herbed to enhance the flavour of the fish.

POLLACK

Pollack is closely related to cod, although it is usually smaller and its flavour is not as good. Most is frozen aboard fishing boats. It is cooked in the same way as cod and is ideal in mixed fish soups.

RED SNAPPER

This large fish, identified by its vivid rose-pink skin and red eyes, has white, creamy flesh and is cut into fillets or cutlets, which can be fried, grilled, poached or steamed. Small ones can be stuffed and baked whole.

SARDINE/PILCHARD

These oily, strong-flavoured fish vary in size. The smaller fish are called sardines, whereas the larger, mature fish are known as pilchards, three or four of which make one serving. Sold fresh, they can be fried, grilled or baked. Canned sardines can be eaten whole as the preserving process softens their bones.

DOLPHIN FISH/ MAHI-MAHI/ DORADO

Found in warm waters, this is a stunningly attractive fish with a streamlined silver body and black and gold spots, which fade once it is caught. Small fish are sold whole, whereas larger fish are sold in cutlets and fillets. Its flesh is firm and well flavoured, and it is very versatile as it can be fried, grilled and cooked in a pie.

SWORDFISH

Swordfish is an enormous fish and is sold as cutlets or chunks. Its firm, dense texture makes it perfect for grilling and frying, although it can also be poached, steamed or baked.

TUNA

There are many species of this large fish, with its dark blue back and silver-grey sides and belly, including skipjack, yellowfin, bluefin, albacore and big-eye. Its flesh varies in colour from pale pink to dark red and it has a firm, dense texture. It can be bought in chunks or steaks, for frying, grilling, braising or poaching, but it should not be overcooked as it tends to dry out during cooking. Tuna is also sold canned in oil, brine or spring water.

POMPANO

This warmwater fish has a silver skin and fatty flesh. It can be bought whole or in fillets. Its skin should be removed before cooking. It can be baked, fried, grilled, steamed, poached or used in soups and stews.

CONGER EEL/ MORAY EEL

These are snake-like fish whose bodies can grow up to 2.5 metres/8 feet. The conger eel was once part of the staple diet of the Cornish people, as it was easily caught along the rocky coastline of southern England. It is also available smoked. The moray eel, of which there are several species, is a cousin of the conger eel, but is much smaller. Both conger and moray eels have firm, white flesh and are usually sold in cutlets. They can be roasted or baked and are good in pies, soups and stews.

ANCHOVY

These small fish are identified by their large mouths, which almost stretch back to their gills. They are high in fat and, although occasionally available fresh, most are filleted, cured in salt and oil and then canned. They are sold flat or rolled.

LING

Ling, with its long, brown, eel-like body, is the largest member of the cod family and has soft, white flesh. It is seldom available fresh, but is usually either salted or smoked.

SPRAT

Sprat is now rarely sold fresh, but is available smoked. It is very similar to a small herring and can be used in the same way.

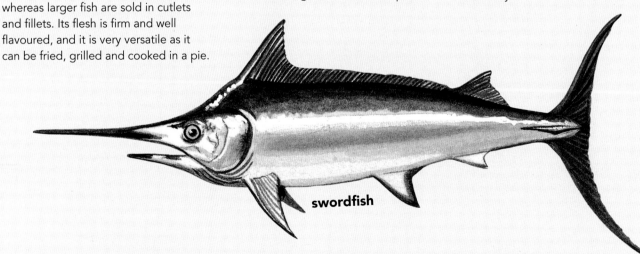

swordfish

red snapper

sardine

pompano

anchovy

tuna

TRIMMING AND SCALING A ROUND SEAFISH

Before preparing fish it must be cleaned. This means removing the entrails and gills and sometimes the scales and fins. Your fish supplier with often do this for you, otherwise the following guidelines provide a step-by-step method.

Trimming round seafish

If desired, using kitchen scissors, cut off the gills and fins if the fish is to be served whole. The head and tail may also be cut off using a sharp knife. Rinse the cavity under cold running water. Fins and scales don't need to be removed if the fish is to be filleted or the skin is to be removed after cooking, or in the case of trout, where the scales are part of the skin.

Scaling round seafish

This is necessary for fish such as sea bass, salmon and snapper. Using the back of a knife or a fish scaler, scrape from the tail to the head, away from the direction of the scales, in short, firm strokes. As scales have a tendency to fly everywhere, you might find this easier if you put the fish in the sink, either in a large polythene bag or covered with a large tea towel. Rinse under cold running water and dry on kitchen paper.

GRILLED RED SNAPPER WITH GARLIC (SEE PAGE 96)

GUTTING AND POCKET-GUTTING A ROUND SEAFISH

Although your fish supplier should do this for you, it's a useful technique to learn, as you may be lucky enough to buy your fish straight from the boat or even catch your own!

Gutting round seafish

1 To remove the entrails, make a slit along the belly from the gills to the tail vent. Pull out the insides and clean away any blood in the cavity.

2 Remove the kidneys by running your thumbnail along the underside of the spine.

3 Rub with a little salt to remove the black skin. Rinse under cold water and dry with kitchen paper.

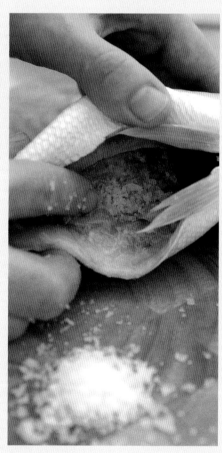

Pocket-gutting round seafish

This is suitable for creating a pocket in a fish while keeping the body intact. The fish is gutted through the gills, but it is not as simple a method as gutting a round seafish along its belly.

1 Using a sharp knife, cut the end of the gut away from the anus, then open the gill covering and make a slit to reveal the throat.

2 With your fingers, pull out the guts through the throat cavity. Rinse under cold water, removing any remaining innards, and dry on kitchen paper.

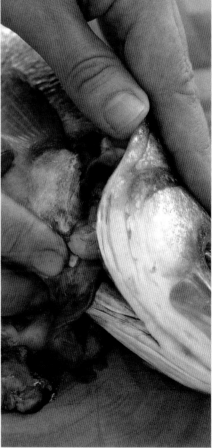

FILLETING LARGE AND SMALL ROUND SEAFISH

Very large round fish, such as John Dory, can be filleted into four, following the flat fish method, or the whole sides can be lifted as described here and then each cut into two fillets. Butterfly boning is a suitable filleting method for small fish such as herrings and sardines that are usually cooked whole.

Filleting small round seafish

1 Cut off the head and fins. Make a slit along the belly from the gills to the tail vent and remove the guts. Rinse under cold running water. Put the fish, skin side up, on a chopping board and, with the heel of your hand, press firmly down on the backbone to loosen it.

Filleting large round seafish

1 Put the fish on its side on a chopping board, with its tail and backbone towards you. Make an angular cut around the gills to the top of the head. It is not necessary to remove either the head or the tail.

2 Cut along the backbone from the head to the tail in order to expose the backbone.

2 Turn the fish over, cut the backbone near the head, then ease the backbone out with your fingers. Remove any pinbones, as described in Pinboning Fish (see page 77), then cut off the tail.

3 With smooth cutting strokes, working from head to tail, separate the flesh from the bones. Turn the flesh over and repeat on the other side, but this time working from tail to head.

RED MULLET COOKED IN A PARCEL (SEE PAGE 107)

SKINNING AND PINBONING WHOLE ROUND SEAFISH AND FISH FILLETS

Whole round seafish are usually cooked with the skin on, which is then removed before serving. The cooking process makes the skin easier to remove, but you must take great care not to damage the soft cooked flesh while removing the skin. Fish fillets are often skinned raw.

Skinning whole round seafish

1 With the point of the knife, loosen the skin under the head. Then, with salted fingers, gently pull the skin down towards the tail, being careful not to break the flesh. Turn the fish over and repeat on the other side.

2 Should you wish to remove the skin before cooking, using a sharp knife, cut along the backbone and across the skin just below the head.

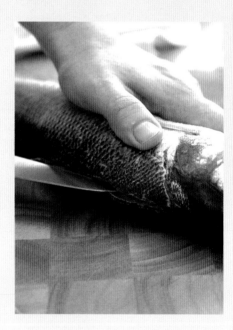

Skinning fish fillets

Put the fish fillet, skin side down, on a chopping board. Gripping the fillet firmly in one hand with a cloth or kitchen paper and with a knife held at an angle, remove the flesh by making a gentle sawing action away from you. A large pinch of salt may help you to grip the fish.

Pinboning fish

Small pinbones are to be found at the top of the flesh of round fish fillets. To remove them, feel for the bones with your fingertips and then remove them using a pair of tweezers.

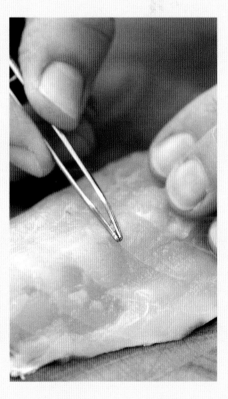

HADDOCK & POTATO SOUP

SERVES 4

INGREDIENTS

- 2 TBSP BUTTER
- 1 ONION, CHOPPED
- 1 LEEK, CHOPPED
- 2 TBSP PLAIN FLOUR
- 850 ML/1½ PINTS MILK
- 1 BAY LEAF
- 2 TBSP CHOPPED FRESH PARSLEY, PLUS EXTRA TO GARNISH
- 350 G/12 OZ SMOKED HADDOCK FILLETS, SKINNED
- 450 G/1 LB POTATOES, COOKED AND MASHED
- 6 TBSP DOUBLE CREAM
- SALT AND PEPPER
- FRESH CRUSTY ROLLS, TO SERVE

1 Melt the butter in a large saucepan over a medium heat, add the onion and leek and cook, stirring frequently, for 3 minutes, or until slightly soft. Mix the flour in a bowl with enough of the milk to make a smooth paste, then stir into the saucepan. Cook, stirring constantly, for 2 minutes, then gradually stir in the remaining milk. Add the bay leaf and parsley and season to taste with salt and pepper. Bring to the boil, then reduce the heat and simmer for 15 minutes.

2 Rinse the haddock fillets under cold running water, drain, then cut into bite-sized chunks. Add to the soup and cook for 15 minutes, or until the fish is tender and cooked right through. Add the mashed potatoes and stir in the cream. Cook for a further 2–3 minutes, then remove from the heat and remove and discard the bay leaf.

3 Ladle into warmed serving bowls, garnish with chopped parsley and serve with crusty rolls.

MEXICAN FISH & ROASTED TOMATO SOUP

SERVES 4

INGREDIENTS

- 5 RIPE TOMATOES
- 5 GARLIC CLOVES, UNPEELED
- 1 LITRE/1¾ PINTS FISH STOCK (SEE PAGE 22)
- 500 G/1 LB 2 OZ RED SNAPPER FILLETS, SKINNED AND CUT INTO CHUNKS
- 2–3 TBSP OLIVE OIL
- 1 ONION, CHOPPED
- 2 FRESH GREEN CHILLIES, DESEEDED AND THINLY SLICED
- LIME WEDGES, TO SERVE (OPTIONAL)

1 Heat a dry, heavy-based frying pan over a high heat, add the tomatoes and garlic cloves and cook, turning frequently, for 10–15 minutes until the skins are blackened and charred and the flesh is tender, or cook under a preheated hot grill. Alternatively, put the tomatoes and garlic cloves in a roasting tin and bake in a preheated oven at 200°C/400°F/Gas Mark 6 for 40 minutes.

2 Leave the tomatoes and garlic to cool, then remove and discard the skins and roughly chop the flesh, combining it with any juices from the pan. Set aside.

3 Heat the stock in a saucepan over a medium heat until simmering, add the fish and cook just until opaque and slightly firm. Remove from the heat and set aside.

4 Heat the oil in a separate saucepan, add the onion and cook, stirring frequently, for 5 minutes, until soft. Strain in the fish cooking liquid, then add the tomatoes and garlic and stir well.

5 Bring to the boil, then reduce the heat and simmer for 5 minutes to combine the flavours. Add the chillies.

6 Divide chunks of the poached fish between 4 soup bowls, ladle over the hot soup and serve with the lime wedges for squeezing over, if using.

SMOKED COD CHOWDER

SERVES 4

INGREDIENTS

- 25 G/1 OZ BUTTER
- 1 ONION, FINELY CHOPPED
- 1 SMALL CELERY STICK, FINELY DICED
- 250 G/9 OZ POTATOES, DICED
- 55 G/2 OZ CARROTS, DICED
- 300 ML/10 FL OZ BOILING WATER
- 350 G/12 OZ SMOKED COD FILLETS, SKINNED AND CUT INTO BITE-SIZED PIECES
- 300 ML/10 FL OZ MILK
- SALT AND PEPPER
- FRESH FLAT-LEAF PARSLEY SPRIGS, TO GARNISH

1 Melt the butter in a large saucepan over a low heat, add the onion and celery and cook, stirring frequently, for 5 minutes, or until soft but not brown.

2 Add the potatoes, carrots, water and salt and pepper to taste. Bring to the boil, then reduce the heat and simmer for 10 minutes, or until the vegetables are tender. Add the fish to the chowder and cook for a further 10 minutes.

3 Pour in the milk and heat gently. Taste and adjust the seasoning, if necessary. Serve hot, in warmed soup bowls, garnished with the parsley sprigs.

ROASTED SALMON WITH
LEMON & HERBS

SERVES 4

INGREDIENTS

- 6 TBSP EXTRA VIRGIN OLIVE OIL
- 1 ONION, SLICED
- 1 LEEK, TRIMMED AND SLICED
- JUICE OF ½ LEMON
- 2 TBSP CHOPPED FRESH
  PARSLEY
- 2 TBSP CHOPPED FRESH DILL
- 500 G/1 LB 2 OZ SALMON
  FILLETS
- SALT AND PEPPER
- FRESHLY COOKED BABY
  SPINACH LEAVES AND LEMON
  WEDGES, TO SERVE

1 Preheat the oven to 200°C/400°F/Gas Mark 6. Heat 1 tablespoon of the oil in a frying pan over a medium heat. Add the onion and leek and cook, stirring, for about 4 minutes until slightly soft.

2 Meanwhile, put the remaining oil in a small bowl with the lemon juice and herbs, and season. Stir together well. Rinse the fish under cold running water, then pat dry with kitchen paper. Arrange the fish in a shallow, ovenproof baking dish.

3 Remove the frying pan from the heat and spread the onion and leek over the fish. Pour the oil mixture over the top, ensuring that everything is well coated. Roast in the centre of the preheated oven for about 10 minutes or until the fish is cooked through.

4 Arrange the cooked spinach on warmed serving plates. Remove the fish and vegetables from the oven and arrange on top of the spinach. Serve immediately, accompanied by the lemon wedges.

TUNA STEAKS WITH CATALAN SAUCE

SERVES 4

INGREDIENTS

- 2 TBSP OLIVE OIL, PLUS EXTRA FOR BRUSHING
- 1 ONION, CHOPPED
- 2 RED PEPPERS, DESEEDED AND CHOPPED
- 1 FRESH RED CHILLI, DESEEDED AND CHOPPED
- 1 GARLIC CLOVE, CHOPPED
- 400 G/14 OZ CANNED CHOPPED TOMATOES
- DASH OF WHITE WINE VINEGAR
- 50 G/1¾ OZ GROUND ALMONDS
- 4 TUNA STEAKS, EACH ABOUT 125 G/4½ OZ
- SALT AND PEPPER
- COOKED FRENCH BEANS AND LEMON WEDGES, TO SERVE

1 Heat the oil in a non-stick frying pan over a medium–high heat. Add the onion and peppers and cook, stirring frequently, for 10 minutes, or until soft. Add the chilli and garlic and cook, stirring, for 1 minute. Add the tomatoes and their juice, bring to a simmer and cook for 15 minutes. Stir in the vinegar.

2 Transfer the tomato mixture to a blender or food processor. Add the ground almonds and blend for 20 seconds, or until smooth. Season with a little salt and pepper to taste, and add a little water if the mixture is too thick to pour.

3 Preheat the grill to high or heat a ridged griddle pan over a high heat. Rinse the tuna under cold running water and pat dry with kitchen paper. Lightly brush with oil on both sides. Cook under the preheated grill or in the very hot griddle pan for 2 minutes on each side, or according to your taste, but do not overcook.

4 Transfer the tuna steaks to warmed plates and spoon over the sauce. Serve immediately with French beans and lemon wedges.

BAKED LEMON COD
WITH HERB SAUCE

SERVES 4

INGREDIENTS

- 4 THICK COD FILLETS
- OLIVE OIL, FOR BRUSHING
- 8 THIN LEMON SLICES
- SALT AND PEPPER
- COOKED FRENCH BEANS, TO SERVE

HERB SAUCE

- 4 TBSP OLIVE OIL
- 1 GARLIC CLOVE, CRUSHED
- 4 TBSP CHOPPED FRESH PARSLEY
- 2 TBSP CHOPPED FRESH MINT
- JUICE OF ½ LEMON
- SALT AND PEPPER

1 Preheat the oven to 200°C/400°F/Gas Mark 6. Rinse each cod fillet and pat dry with kitchen paper, then brush with oil. Place each fillet on a piece of baking paper large enough to encase the fish in a parcel. Top each fillet with 2 lemon slices and season to taste with salt and pepper. Fold over the baking paper to encase the fish and bake in the preheated oven for 20 minutes, or until just cooked and opaque.

2 Meanwhile, to make the herb sauce, put all the ingredients into a food processor and process until finely chopped. Season to taste with salt and pepper.

3 Carefully unfold each parcel and place on a serving plate. Pour a spoonful of herb sauce over each piece of fish before serving, accompanied by the French beans.

FISH & CHIPS

SERVES 2

INGREDIENTS

- VEGETABLE OIL, FOR DEEP-FRYING
- 3 LARGE POTATOES, SUCH AS CARA OR DESIRÉE
- 2 THICK COD OR HADDOCK FILLETS, 175 G/6 OZ EACH
- 175 G/6 OZ SELF-RAISING FLOUR, PLUS EXTRA FOR DUSTING
- 200 ML/7 FL OZ COLD LAGER
- SALT AND PEPPER
- SPRIGS OF FRESH FLAT-LEAF PARSLEY, TO GARNISH
- TARTARE SAUCE, TO SERVE (SEE PAGE 24)

1 Heat the oil in a temperature-controlled deep-fat fryer to 120°C/250°F, or in a heavy-based saucepan, checking the temperature with a thermometer, to blanch the chips. Preheat the oven to 150°C/300°F/Gas Mark 2.

2 Peel the potatoes and cut into even-sized chips. Fry for about 8–10 minutes, depending on size, until soft but not coloured. Remove from the oil, drain on kitchen paper and place in a warm dish in the preheated oven. Increase the temperature of the oil to 180°C/350°F, or until a cube of bread browns in 30 seconds.

3 Meanwhile, season the fish with salt and pepper and dust it lightly with a little flour.

4 Make a thick batter by sifting the flour into a bowl with a little salt and whisking in most of the lager. Check the consistency before adding the remainder: it should be very thick like double cream.

5 Dip one fillet into the batter and allow the batter to coat it thickly. Carefully place the fish in the hot oil, then repeat with the other fillet.

6 Cook for 8–10 minutes, depending on the thickness of the fish. Turn the fillets over halfway through the cooking time. Remove the fish from the fryer, drain and keep warm.

7 Make sure the oil temperature is still at 180°C/350°F and return the chips to the fryer. Cook for a further 2–3 minutes until golden brown and crispy. Drain and season with salt and pepper before serving with the battered fish and some Tartare Sauce, garnished with parsley.

STEAMED SEA BREAM WITH GINGER

SERVES 4

INGREDIENTS

- 500 G/1 LB 2 OZ SEA BREAM OR PERCH FILLETS
- 1 GARLIC CLOVE, FINELY CHOPPED
- 1 SMALL RED CHILLI, DESEEDED AND FINELY CHOPPED
- 2 TBSP THAI FISH SAUCE (NAM PLA)
- 3 TBSP LEMON JUICE
- 100 ML/3½ FL OZ FISH STOCK (SEE PAGE 22)
- 3 SPRING ONIONS, TRIMMED AND FINELY SLICED
- 1 TBSP FINELY GRATED LEMON RIND
- 1 TBSP FINELY GRATED FRESH GINGER
- SPRIGS OF FRESH CORIANDER, TO GARNISH

TO SERVE
- FRESHLY COOKED EGG NOODLES
- LEMON WEDGES
- FRESH BREAD ROLLS (OPTIONAL)

1 Rinse the fish fillets under cold running water, then pat dry with kitchen paper. Make several fairly deep diagonal cuts into the fish on both sides. Put the fish on a heatproof plate that is slightly smaller than your wok. The plate should have a rim.

2 In a separate bowl, mix together the garlic, chilli, fish sauce, lemon juice and stock. Pour this mixture over the fish. Scatter over the spring onions, lemon rind and ginger.

3 Fill a large wok with boiling water up to a depth of about 4 cm/1½ inches. Bring it back to the boil, then set a rack or trivet inside the wok. Put the plate of fish on top of the rack, then cover the wok with a lid. Reduce the heat a little and steam the fish for about 10 minutes, or until cooked through.

4 Lift out the fish and arrange on the freshly cooked egg noodles. Garnish with the coriander sprigs, and serve with the noodles, lemon wedges and the fresh bread rolls, if using.

GRILLED MAHI MAHI WITH TOMATO & OLIVE SAUCE

SERVES 4

INGREDIENTS

- 4 TBSP OLIVE OIL
- 1 RED ONION, FINELY CHOPPED
- 2 GARLIC CLOVES, FINELY CHOPPED
- 1 RED PEPPER, DESEEDED AND CHOPPED
- 2 TBSP DRY WHITE WINE
- 350 G/12 OZ PLUM TOMATOES, PEELED AND CHOPPED
- 1 TBSP CHOPPED FRESH FLAT-LEAF PARSLEY
- 1 TSP CHOPPED FRESH THYME
- 1 BAY LEAF
- 700 G/1 LB 9 OZ MAHI MAHI FILLETS, SKINNED
- 12 BLACK OLIVES, STONED AND CHOPPED
- SALT AND PEPPER
- FRESH FLAT-LEAF PARSLEY SPRIGS, TO GARNISH

1 Heat half the olive oil in a heavy-based saucepan. Add the onion, garlic and red pepper and cook over a low heat, stirring occasionally, for 10 minutes, until soft but not coloured.

2 Stir in the wine, increase the heat to medium and cook until the liquid has reduced by half. Add the tomatoes, parsley, thyme and bay leaf and season to taste with salt and pepper. Bring to the boil, then reduce the heat, cover and simmer for 10 minutes.

3 Meanwhile, preheat the grill to medium–hot. Place the fish fillets in a bowl. Add the remaining oil, season with salt and pepper and toss well to coat. Spread out the fish on a baking tray.

4 Stir the olives into the tomato sauce, re-cover the pan and simmer while you cook the fish. Place the fish under the grill and cook, without turning, for 2–4 minutes, until the flesh flakes easily.

5 Divide the sauce between 4 warmed plates, top with the fish and garnish with the parsley sprigs. Serve immediately.

GRILLED RED SNAPPER WITH GARLIC

SERVES 4

INGREDIENTS

- 2 TBSP LEMON JUICE
- 4 TBSP OLIVE OIL, PLUS EXTRA FOR OILING
- 4 RED SNAPPER OR MULLET, SCALED AND GUTTED
- 2 TBSP CHOPPED FRESH HERBS SUCH AS OREGANO, MARJORAM, FLAT-LEAF PARSLEY OR THYME
- SALT AND PEPPER
- 2 GARLIC CLOVES, FINELY CHOPPED
- 2 TBSP CHOPPED FRESH FLAT-LEAF PARSLEY, TO GARNISH
- LEMON WEDGES AND MIXED SALAD LEAVES, TO SERVE

1 Preheat the grill to medium. Oil the grill pan. Put the lemon juice, oil, and salt and pepper in a bowl and whisk together. Brush the mixture inside and outside the fish and sprinkle over the chopped herbs. Place on the prepared grill pan.

2 Cook the fish under the grill for about 10 minutes, basting frequently and turning once, until golden brown.

3 Meanwhile, mix together the chopped garlic and chopped parsley. Sprinkle the garlic mixture over the cooked fish and serve hot or cold, accompanied by the lemon wedges and salad leaves.

TERIYAKI SALMON FILLETS WITH CHINESE NOODLES

SERVES 4

INGREDIENTS

- 4 SALMON FILLETS, ABOUT 200 G/7 OZ EACH
- 125 ML/4 FL OZ TERIYAKI MARINADE
- 1 SHALLOT, SLICED
- 2-CM/¾-INCH PIECE FRESH GINGER, FINELY CHOPPED
- 2 CARROTS, SLICED
- 115 G/4 OZ CLOSED-CUP MUSHROOMS, SLICED
- 1.2 LITRES/2 PINTS VEGETABLE STOCK
- 250 G/9 OZ DRIED MEDIUM EGG NOODLES
- 115 G/4 OZ FROZEN PEAS
- 175 G/6 OZ CHINESE LEAVES, SHREDDED
- 4 SPRING ONIONS, SLICED

1 Wipe off any fish scales from the salmon skin. Arrange the salmon fillets, skin side up, in a dish just large enough to fit them in a single layer. Mix the teriyaki marinade with the shallot and ginger in a small bowl and pour over the salmon. Cover and leave to marinate in the refrigerator for at least 1 hour, turning the salmon over halfway through the marinating time.

2 Put the carrots, mushrooms and stock into a large saucepan. Arrange the salmon, skin side down, on a shallow baking tray. Pour the fish marinade into the pan of vegetables and stock and bring to the boil. Reduce the heat, cover and simmer for 10 minutes.

3 Meanwhile, preheat the grill to medium. Cook the salmon under the preheated grill for 10–15 minutes, depending on the thickness of the fillets, until the flesh turns pink and flakes easily. Remove from under the grill and keep warm.

4 Add the noodles and peas to the stock and return to the boil. Reduce the heat, cover and simmer for 5 minutes, or until the noodles are tender. Stir in the Chinese leaves and spring onions and heat through for 1 minute.

5 Carefully drain off 300 ml/10 fl oz of the stock into a small heatproof jug and reserve. Drain and discard the remaining stock. Divide the noodles and vegetables between 4 warmed serving bowls and top each with a salmon fillet. Pour the reserved stock over each meal and serve immediately.

BAKED MACKEREL STUFFED WITH RAISINS & PINE KERNELS

SERVES 4

INGREDIENTS

- 3 TBSP OLIVE OIL
- 1 ONION, FINELY CHOPPED
- 100 G/3½ OZ FRESH BREADCRUMBS
- 55 G/2 OZ RAISINS, CHOPPED
- 100 G/3½ OZ PINE KERNELS
- GRATED RIND AND JUICE OF 1 LEMON
- 1 TBSP CHOPPED FRESH DILL
- 2 TBSP CHOPPED FRESH FLAT-LEAF PARSLEY
- 1 EGG, BEATEN
- 4 MACKEREL, EACH WEIGHING ABOUT 350 G/12 OZ, GUTTED
- SALT AND PEPPER
- SPRIGS OF FRESH FLAT-LEAF PARSLEY, TO GARNISH
- LEMON WEDGES, TO SERVE

1 To make the stuffing, heat 2 tablespoons of the oil in a large, heavy-based frying pan, add the onion and fry for 5 minutes, until soft. Remove from the heat.

2 Put the breadcrumbs, raisins, pine kernels, lemon rind, dill, parsley, and salt and pepper to taste, in a large bowl. Add the onion and egg and mix well together.

3 Press the stuffing mixture into the cavity of the fish and place in a greased, shallow ovenproof dish large enough to hold them in a single layer. Using a sharp knife, make diagonal slashes along each fish. Drizzle over the lemon juice and the remaining oil.

4 Bake the fish, uncovered, in a preheated oven, 190°C/ 375°F/ Gas Mark 5, for 30-45 minutes, basting twice during cooking, until tender. Serve hot, garnished with the parsley and accompanied by the lemon wedges.

SWEET & SOUR SEA BASS

SERVES 2

INGREDIENTS

- 60 G/2¼ OZ PAK CHOI, SHREDDED
- 40 G/1½ OZ BEANSPROUTS
- 40 G/1½ OZ SHIITAKE MUSHROOMS, SLICED
- 40 G/1½ OZ OYSTER MUSHROOMS, TORN
- 20 G/¾ OZ SPRING ONION, FINELY SLICED
- 1 TSP FINELY GRATED FRESH GINGER
- 1 TBSP FINELY SLICED LEMON GRASS
- 2 X 90 G/3¼ OZ SEA BASS FILLETS, SKINNED AND BONED
- 10 G/¼ OZ SESAME SEEDS, TOASTED

SWEET & SOUR SAUCE

- 90 ML/3 FL OZ UNSWEETENED PINEAPPLE JUICE
- 1 TBSP SUGAR
- 1 TBSP RED WINE VINEGAR
- 2 STAR ANISE, CRUSHED
- 90 ML/3 FL OZ TOMATO JUICE
- 1 TBSP CORNFLOUR, BLENDED WITH A LITTLE COLD WATER

1 Preheat the oven to 200°C/400°F/ Gas Mark 6. Cut out two 38-cm/15-inch squares of greaseproof paper and two 38-cm/15-inch squares of foil.

2 To make the sauce, heat the pineapple juice, sugar, red wine vinegar, star anise and tomato juice and simmer for 1–2 minutes. Thicken with the cornflour and water mixture, whisking constantly, then pass through a fine sieve into a small bowl to cool.

3 In a separate large bowl mix together the pak choi, beansprouts, mushrooms and spring onions, then add the ginger and lemon grass. Toss all the ingredients together.

4 Put a square of greaseproof paper on top of a square of foil and fold into a triangle. Open up and place half the vegetable mix in the centre, pour half the sweet and sour sauce over the vegetables and place the sea bass on top. Sprinkle with a few sesame seeds. Close the triangle over the mixture and, starting at the top, fold the right corner and crumple the edges together to form an airtight triangular bag. Repeat to make the second bag.

5 Place the foil bags on a baking tray and cook in the oven for 10 minutes until they puff with steam. To serve, place the bags on individual plates and snip them open at the table so that you can enjoy the wonderful aromas as they are opened.

SERVES 4

INGREDIENTS

- 4 X 85 G/3 OZ SNAPPER FILLETS
- VEGETABLE OIL SPRAY
- LEMON WEDGES (OPTIONAL) AND ROCKET LEAVES, TO SERVE

SWEETCORN & PAWPAW RELISH

- 2 TBSP FINELY CHOPPED ONION
- 1 TSP SUGAR
- 22 TBSP WHITE WINE VINEGAR
- 2 TBSP COOKED OR CANNED SWEETCORN KERNELS
- ¼ TSP FINELY CHOPPED HABANERO CHILLI OR OTHER TYPE OF CHILLI
- 100 ML/3½ FL OZ WATER
- ¼ TSP YELLOW MUSTARD SEEDS
- PINCH OF GROUND TURMERIC
- 1 TSP CORNFLOUR, BLENDED WITH A LITTLE COLD WATER
- 50 G/1¾ OZ PAWPAW, CUT INTO 5-MM/¼-INCH CUBES

SEASONING MIX

- ¼ TSP PAPRIKA
- ½ TSP ONION POWDER
- ¼ TSP DRIED THYME
- ¼ TSP DRIED OREGANO
- ¼ TSP CAYENNE PEPPER
- ¼ TSP PEPPER
- ½ TSP CORNFLOUR

BLACKENED SNAPPER WITH SWEETCORN & PAWPAW RELISH

1 To make the relish, place the onion, sugar, vinegar, sweetcorn, chilli, water, mustard seeds and turmeric in a small saucepan over a medium heat and bring to the boil. Simmer for 10 minutes, then add the cornflour mixture, stirring constantly, and cook until it is the required consistency (it will thicken slightly when cooled). Stir in the pawpaw and leave to cool.

2 To make the seasoning mix, put all the ingredients into a small bowl and mix thoroughly.

3 Sprinkle the seasoning mix over the snapper fillets on both sides and pat into the flesh, then shake off any excess. Lay the fillets on a board.

4 Heat a non-stick frying pan over a high heat until smoking. Lightly spray both sides of the fillets with oil, then put into the hot pan and cook for 2 minutes. Turn the fillets and cook all the way through. (If the fillets are thick, finish the cooking under a preheated grill as the less intense heat will prevent the seasoning mix burning.) Remove the fish from the pan.

5 Serve the fillets, topped with relish, on warmed plates, with the lemon wedges, if using, and the rocket leaves.

RED MULLET COOKED IN A PARCEL

SERVES 4

INGREDIENTS

- 4 TBSP EXTRA VIRGIN OLIVE OIL, PLUS EXTRA FOR BRUSHING
- 4 X 280 G/10 OZ RED MULLETS, CLEANED AND SCALED
- 4 GARLIC CLOVES, SLICED THINLY LENGTHWAYS
- 4 TOMATOES, PEELED, DESEEDED AND DICED
- 2 TSP FINELY CHOPPED FRESH ROSEMARY
- SALT AND PEPPER
- SPRIGS OF FRESH FLAT-LEAF PARSLEY AND THINLY SLICED REDS ONIONS, TO GARNISH
- FRESH BREAD, TO SERVE

1 Preheat the oven to 200°C/400°F/Gas Mark 6. Cut out 4 squares of greaseproof paper large enough to enclose the fish and brush with a little olive oil.

2 Rinse the fish inside and out under cold running water, pat dry with kitchen paper and season to taste. Using a sharp knife, cut 3 diagonal slits in both sides of each fish. Insert the garlic slices into the slits.

3 Combine the olive oil, tomatoes and rosemary in a bowl. Spoon a little of the mixture onto each of the greaseproof paper squares, then place the fish on top. Divide the remaining tomato mixture between the fish.

4 Fold up the paper around the fish, twisting it into tiny pleats to seal securely. Place the parcels on a baking tray and bake in the preheated oven for 15 minutes.

5 Transfer the parcels to warmed plates and cut off the folded edges of the parcels. Garnish with the parsley sprigs and red onion slices and serve with the bread.

FLAKY PASTRY FISH PIE

SERVES 4–6

INGREDIENTS

- 650 G/1 LB 7 OZ WHITE FISH FILLETS, SUCH AS COD OR HADDOCK, SKINNED
- 300 ML/10 FL OZ MILK
- 1 BAY LEAF
- 4 PEPPERCORNS
- 1 SMALL ONION, FINELY SLICED
- 40 G/1½ OZ BUTTER, PLUS EXTRA FOR GREASING
- 40 G/1½ OZ PLAIN FLOUR, PLUS EXTRA FOR DUSTING
- 1 TBSP CHOPPED FRESH PARSLEY OR TARRAGON
- 150 ML/5 FL OZ SINGLE CREAM
- 2 HARD-BOILED EGGS, ROUGHLY CHOPPED
- 400 G/14 OZ READY-MADE PUFF PASTRY
- 1 EGG, BEATEN
- SALT AND PEPPER

1 Preheat the oven to 200°C/400°F/Gas Mark 6. Grease a 1.2-litre/2-pint pie dish.

2 Put the fish in a frying pan and cover with the milk. Add the bay leaf, peppercorns and onion slices. Bring to the boil, then reduce the heat and simmer gently for 10–12 minutes.

3 Remove from the heat and strain off the milk into a measuring jug. Add a little extra milk, if necessary, to make up to 300 ml/10 fl oz. Flake the fish into large pieces, removing and discarding any bones.

4 Melt the butter in a saucepan over a low heat, add the flour and cook, stirring constantly, for 2–3 minutes. Remove from the heat and gradually stir in the reserved milk, beating well after each addition. Return the saucepan to the heat and cook, stirring constantly, until thickened. Cook for a further 2–3 minutes until smooth and glossy. Add the herbs, cream, and salt and pepper to taste.

5 Put the fish in the pie dish, then add the hard-boiled eggs and season to taste with salt and pepper. Pour the sauce over the fish and mix carefully.

6 Roll out the pastry on a lightly floured work surface until just larger than the pie dish. Cut off a strip 1 cm/½ inch wide from around the edge. Moisten the rim of the dish with water and press the pastry strip onto it. Moisten the pastry collar and put on the pastry lid. Crimp the edges to seal well. If desired, garnish with the pastry trimmings shaped into leaves. Brush with the beaten egg.

7 Put the pie on a baking tray and bake near the top of the preheated oven for 20–25 minutes. Cover with foil if it begins to get too brown.

WARM TUNA & KIDNEY BEAN SALAD

SERVES 4

INGREDIENTS

- 4 TUNA STEAKS, EACH ABOUT 175 G/6 OZ
- 1 TBSP OLIVE OIL
- 200 G/7 OZ CANNED KIDNEY BEANS, DRAINED AND RINSED
- 100 G/3½ OZ CANNED SWEETCORN, DRAINED
- 2 SPRING ONIONS, TRIMMED AND THINLY SLICED
- SALT AND PEPPER
- LIME WEDGES, TO GARNISH

DRESSING

- 5 TBSP EXTRA VIRGIN OLIVE OIL
- 3 TBSP BALSAMIC VINEGAR
- 1 TBSP LIME JUICE
- 1 GARLIC CLOVE, CHOPPED
- 1 TBSP CHOPPED FRESH CORIANDER
- SALT AND PEPPER

1 Preheat a ridged griddle pan. Rinse the tuna under cold running water and pat dry with kitchen paper. Brush the tuna steaks with olive oil, then season to taste with salt and pepper.

2 Cook the tuna in the preheated griddle pan for 2 minutes, then turn over and cook on the other side for a further 2 minutes, or according to your taste, but do not overcook. Remove from the heat and allow to cool slightly.

3 To make the dressing, put all the ingredients into a small bowl and stir together well.

4 Put the kidney beans, sweetcorn and spring onions into a large bowl, pour over half of the dressing and mix together well. Divide the bean and sweetcorn salad among individual serving plates, then place a tuna steak on each one. Drizzle over the remaining dressing, garnish with lime wedges and serve immediately.

SPICY JOHN DORY

SERVES 4

INGREDIENTS

- 2 JOHN DORY, FILLETED
- 2 GARLIC CLOVES, CHOPPED
- 2 SHALLOTS, GRATED
- 1 SMALL FRESH RED CHILLI, DESEEDED AND CHOPPED
- 1 TBSP LEMON JUICE

TO SERVE

- CRISP GREEN SALAD LEAVES
- AÏOLI (SEE PAGE 24)
- GRILLED TOMATO HALVES

1 Preheat the barbecue. Rinse the fish under cold running water and pat dry with kitchen paper. Mix the garlic, shallots, chilli and lemon juice together in a separate bowl. Rub the mixture onto both sides of the fillets.

2 Cook the fish over hot coals for 15 minutes, or until cooked through, turning once. Arrange the fish on a bed of green salad leaves, and serve with the Aïoli and tomatoes.

FRESHWATER FISH

When you're in the mood for something different, give freshwater fish a try. You'll find native trout, along with imported varieties, such as carp, catfish, rockfish and tilapia, at the fish counter, whole or filleted. Freshwater fish are best known for their mild, delicate flavour and the flesh varies from fine to coarse, depending on the species. The skin and a thin layer of fat are often removed before cooking, and these fish are good baked, fried or poached.

THE FRESHWATER FISH DIRECTORY

The following is a guide to all the main species of freshwater fish that can be eaten, listed by their common names, although some fish, confusingly, are known by a variety of different names. The potted profile for each fish details the various forms in which it can be purchased, for example whole or in fillets, fresh or canned, and the most suitable cooking methods.

CATFISH/ROCKFISH

There are many species of catfish, many of which are frozen. It is available whole or as fillets and its tough skin must be removed before cooking. It can be fried, grilled, poached, steamed, baked or used in soups and stews.

TROUT

There are many varieties of trout, including river, brown, rainbow and salmon trout. It is usually cooked whole and can be baked, fried, grilled, poached or steamed. It is also available smoked, in the same way as smoked salmon.

CHAR

Char is similar to trout in size and appearance, but more colourful. Its flesh is firm and usually white, or sometimes pale pink. Arctic char is now commonly available, thanks to farming in Iceland and Canada. It is usually sold filleted and can be fried, baked or steamed.

TILAPIA/ST PETER'S FISH

Farming has made tilapia more widely available and it can now be purchased whole or as fillets. It has a firm texture and is suitable for all cooking methods. An interesting feature of this fish is that the females carry their young in their mouths. They are smaller than the males.

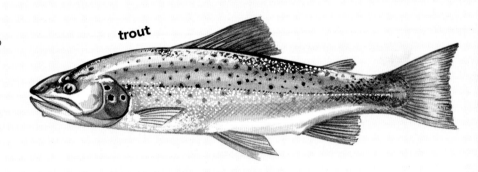

trout

catfish

EEL/COMMON EEL/ ELVER

This snake-like fish, smaller than the seawater conger eel, lives in rivers and streams and then swims thousands of kilometres to return to the sea and spawn, after which it dies (the opposite migratory habit of salmon). Elvers are baby eels and are no longer eaten, but used to restock fisheries. Eels are currently overfished and should be avoided at the present time (see the best choices to make in the Marine Conservation Society Good Fish Guide on page 16–17).

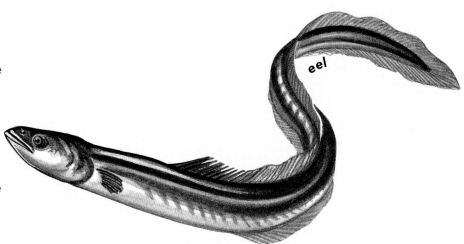

eel

Preparing a fish noisette from a fish cutlet

1 After removing the pinbones (see page 77), using a sharp knife, remove the skin from the flesh halfway around the cutlet.

2 Curl the skinned piece of fish into the centre and wrap the rest of the cutlet around the outside.

3 Wrap the loose piece of skin around the cutlet and secure the whole noisette with wooden cocktail sticks.

POACHED TROUT WITH BUTTER SAUCE

SERVES 4

INGREDIENTS

- 4 RAINBOW TROUT, FINS REMOVED AND GUTTED, WITH HEAD LEFT ON OR REMOVED, RINSED INSIDE AND OUT AND DRIED
- 1.2 LITRES/2 PINTS COURT BOUILLON (SEE PAGE 22)
- 8 LEMON WEDGES AND 8 SPRIGS OF FRESH TARRAGON, TO GARNISH
- BEURRE BLANC (SEE PAGE 25), TO SERVE

1 Put the fish in a sauté or frying pan large enough to hold them side by side. Pour over enough Court Bouillon to cover and slowly bring to the boil. Immediately reduce the heat to very low and leave the fish to simmer for 8–10 minutes until the flesh flakes easily.

2 Remove the fish from the liquid and pat dry. The fish can now be served whole or skinned and filleted. Serve on warmed plates with the Beurre Blanc spooned over, or served in a separate bowl, garnished with the lemon wedges and tarragon sprigs.

TROUT WITH MUSSELS & PRAWNS

SERVES 4

INGREDIENTS

- 30 G/1 OZ BUTTER
- ½ TBSP SUNFLOWER OIL
- 12 BUTTON MUSHROOMS, THINLY SLICED
- 24 LIVE MUSSELS
- 1 SHALLOT, CHOPPED
- 1 GARLIC CLOVE, CRUSHED
- 250 ML/9 FL OZ DRY WHITE WINE
- 24 RAW PRAWNS IN THEIR SHELLS
- 4 TROUT FILLETS, ABOUT 175 G/6 OZ EACH, ALL SKIN AND BONES REMOVED
- 250 ML/9 FL OZ DOUBLE CREAM
- SALT AND PEPPER
- SPRIGS OF FRESH CHERVIL, TO GARNISH

BEURRE MANIÉ
- 15 G/½ OZ UNSALTED BUTTER, SOFTENED
- 15 G/½ OZ PLAIN FLOUR

1 Melt the butter with the oil in a heavy-based frying pan over a medium–high heat. Add the mushrooms and sauté for 5–7 minutes until brown, then set aside.

2 Meanwhile, preheat the oven to 190°C/375°F/Gas Mark 5. Lightly grease an ovenproof dish large enough to hold the trout fillets in a single layer and set aside.

3 To prepare the mussels, cut off and discard any beards, then scrub any dirty shells. Discard any mussels with broken shells or open ones that do not instantly close when tapped.

4 Put the shallot, garlic and wine in a large saucepan with a tight-fitting lid over a high heat and bring to the boil. Reduce the heat to very low. Add the mussels and prawns to the saucepan, cover tightly and simmer for 4 minutes, shaking the pan frequently, or until the mussels open and the prawns turn pink. Discard any mussels that do not open.

5 Line a large sieve with a piece of muslin and place over a large bowl. Tip the contents of the pan into the sieve and strain, reserving the cooking liquid.

6 Remove the mussels from their shells, reserving 4 unshelled mussels for a garnish. Peel the prawns and reserve the shells and heads, then set aside the mussels and prawns.

7 Put the cooking liquid in a small saucepan over a high heat, add the prawn shells and heads and boil for 3 minutes, skimming the surface if necessary.

8 Lay the trout fillets in the prepared dish and strain the cooking juices over. Sprinkle with the sliced mushrooms. Cover the dish with foil, shiny side down, and bake for 10–12 minutes until the trout is tender and flakes easily. Remove the trout, add to the shellfish and cover to keep warm, reserving the cooking liquid.

9 Meanwhile, to make the Beurre Manié, mash the butter and flour together to make a thick paste.

10 To make the sauce, pour the cooking liquid into a small saucepan over a high heat. Bring to the boil, then add small amounts of the Beurre Manié, whisking constantly and adding more only when the previous amount has been incorporated. Continue boiling and whisking until the sauce is thick and shiny. Stir in the cream and boil until the sauce has reduced by half. Add salt and pepper to taste, then stir in the mussels and prawns and just warm through.

11 Transfer the trout fillets to warmed plates and spoon the sauce and shellfish over. Garnish with the chervil and the reserved unshelled mussels.

CREAMY SMOKED TROUT TAGLIATELLE

SERVES 6

INGREDIENTS

- 2 CARROTS, CUT INTO THIN BATONS
- 2 CELERY STICKS, CUT INTO THIN BATONS
- 1 COURGETTE, CUT INTO THIN BATONS
- 1 LEEK, CUT INTO THIN BATONS
- 115 G/4 OZ FRESH OR FROZEN PEAS
- 150 ML/5 FL OZ VEGETABLE STOCK
- 225 G/8 OZ SMOKED TROUT FILLETS, SKINNED AND CUT INTO THIN STRIPS
- 200 G/7 OZ CREAM CHEESE
- 150 ML/5 FL OZ DRY WHITE WINE
- 2 TBSP CHOPPED FRESH DILL, PLUS EXTRA SPRIGS TO GARNISH
- 225 G/8 OZ DRIED TAGLIATELLE
- SALT AND PEPPER

1 Put the carrots, celery, courgette, leek and peas in a large, heavy-based saucepan and pour in the stock. Bring to the boil, then reduce the heat and simmer for 5 minutes, or until the vegetables are tender and most of the stock has evaporated. Remove the pan from the heat, stir in the smoked trout and cover to keep warm.

2 Put the cheese and wine in a separate large, heavy-based saucepan over a low heat and stir until the cheese has melted and the mixture is smooth. Stir in the chopped dill and season to taste with salt and pepper.

3 Meanwhile, bring another large, heavy-based saucepan of lightly salted water to the boil. Add the pasta, return to the boil and cook for 8–10 minutes, until the pasta is tender but still firm to the bite. Drain the pasta and tip into the cheese sauce. Toss the pasta using 2 large forks, then transfer to a warmed serving dish. Top with the smoked trout mixture, garnish with the dill sprigs and serve immediately.

FRIED CATFISH FILLETS

SERVES 4

INGREDIENTS

- 70 G/2½ OZ PLAIN FLOUR
- 2 EGGS
- 225 G/8 OZ POLENTA
- ½ TSP DRIED THYME
- PINCH OF CAYENNE PEPPER
- 900 G/2 LB CATFISH FILLETS, SKINNED, RINSED AND PATTED DRY
- CORN OIL, FOR SHALLOW-FRYING
- SALT AND PEPPER

TO SERVE

- SALAD LEAVES
- LEMON WEDGES
- MAYONNAISE

1 Put the flour on a plate. Beat the eggs in a wide, shallow bowl. Put the polenta on a separate plate and season with the thyme, cayenne pepper, and salt and pepper to taste.

2 Dust the catfish fillets with the seasoned flour on both sides, shaking off any excess, dip into the beaten eggs, then pat the polenta onto both sides.

3 Heat about 5 cm/2 inches of oil in a large frying pan over a medium heat. Add as many catfish fillets as will fit without overcrowding the frying pan and cook for 2 minutes, or until the coating is golden brown.

4 Turn the catfish fillets over and cook for a further 2 minutes, or until the flesh flakes easily. Remove from the frying pan with a slotted spoon and drain on kitchen paper. Transfer the fillets to a low oven to keep warm while cooking the remaining fillets, if necessary. Add more oil to the frying pan as needed.

5 Serve the fried catfish with the salad leaves and lemon wedges, accompanied by some mayonnaise.

DEEP-FRIED RIVER FISH WITH CHILLI BEAN SAUCE

SERVES 4–6

INGREDIENTS

- 1 WHOLE FRESHWATER FISH, SUCH AS TROUT, WEIGHING 400 G/14 OZ, GUTTED
- 1 HEAPED TBSP PLAIN FLOUR
- PINCH OF SALT
- 125 ML/4 FL OZ WATER
- VEGETABLE OR GROUNDNUT OIL, FOR DEEP-FRYING
- SHREDDED SPRING ONION, TO GARNISH

CHILLI BEAN SAUCE

- 125 ML/4 FL OZ VEGETABLE OR GROUNDNUT OIL
- 1 TSP DRIED CHILLI FLAKES
- 1 GARLIC CLOVE, FINELY CHOPPED
- 1 TSP FINELY CHOPPED FRESH GINGER
- 1 TBSP CHILLI BEAN SAUCE
- ½ TSP WHITE PEPPER
- 2 TSP SUGAR
- 1 TBSP WHITE RICE VINEGAR
- 1 TSP FINELY CHOPPED SPRING ONION

1 To prepare the fish, clean and dry thoroughly. Mix together the flour, salt, and water to create a light batter. Coat the fish with the batter.

2 Heat enough oil for deep-frying in a wok, deep-fat fryer or large heavy-based pan until it reaches 180°C/350°F, or until a cube of bread browns in 30 seconds. Deep-fry the fish on one side at a time until the skin is crisp and golden brown. Drain, then set aside and keep warm.

3 To make the sauce, first heat all but 1 tablespoon of the oil in a small saucepan and, when smoking, pour over the dried chilli flakes. Set aside.

4 In a preheated wok or deep saucepan, heat the remaining oil and stir-fry the garlic and ginger until fragrant. Stir in the chilli bean sauce, then add the oil-chilli flake mixture. Season with the pepper, sugar and vinegar. Turn off the heat and stir in the spring onion. Tip the sauce over the fish, garnish with the shredded spring onion and serve immediately.

CATFISH STEW

SERVES 4

INGREDIENTS

- 2 TSP GARLIC GRANULES
- 1 TSP CELERY SALT
- 1 TSP PEPPER
- 1 TSP CURRY POWDER
- 1 TSP PAPRIKA
- PINCH OF CASTER SUGAR
- 4–8 SLICES CATFISH OR ROCKFISH, ABOUT 900 G/2 LB TOTAL WEIGHT
- 2 TBSP RED WINE VINEGAR
- 40 G/1½ OZ PLAIN FLOUR
- 6 TBSP SUNFLOWER OIL
- 1 ONION, FINELY CHOPPED
- 2 GARLIC CLOVES, FINELY CHOPPED
- 280 G/10 OZ TOMATOES, PEELED AND CHOPPED
- 1 FRESH MARJORAM SPRIG
- 600 ML/1 PINT FISH STOCK
- ¼ TSP GROUND CUMIN
- ¼ TSP GROUND CINNAMON
- 2 RED OR GREEN CHILLIES, DESEEDED AND FINELY CHOPPED
- 1 RED PEPPER, DESEEDED AND FINELY CHOPPED
- 1 YELLOW PEPPER, DESEEDED AND FINELY CHOPPED
- SALT
- FRESH CRUSTY BREAD, TO SERVE

1 Mix together the garlic granules, celery salt, pepper, curry powder, paprika and caster sugar in a small bowl. Place the fish in a non-metallic dish and sprinkle with half the spice mixture. Turn the fish over and sprinkle with the remaining spice mixture. Add the vinegar and turn to coat. Cover with clingfilm and set aside in a cool place to marinate for 1 hour.

2 Spread out the flour in a shallow dish. Drain the fish and dip the slices in the flour to coat, shaking off any excess.

3 Heat 4 tablespoons of the oil in a frying pan. Add the fish and cook over a medium heat for 2–3 minutes on each side. Remove with a fish slice and set aside.

4 Wipe out the frying pan with kitchen paper, add the remaining oil and heat. Add the onion and cook over a low heat, stirring occasionally, for 5 minutes, until soft. Add the chopped garlic and cook, stirring, for a further 2 minutes. Add the tomatoes and marjoram, increase the heat to medium and cook, stirring occasionally, for 8 minutes.

5 Stir in the stock, cumin and cinnamon and add the fish, chillies and peppers. Bring to the boil, then reduce the heat and simmer for 8–10 minutes, until the fish flakes easily and the sauce has thickened. Season to taste with salt and serve immediately with fresh crusty bread.

TILAPIA WITH MINT COUSCOUS

SERVES 4

INGREDIENTS
- 4 TBSP OLIVE OIL
- 1 RED ONION, FINELY CHOPPED
- 1 GARLIC CLOVE, FINELY CHOPPED
- 300 ML/10 FL OZ FISH STOCK
- 115 G/4 OZ COUSCOUS
- 2 TBSP CHOPPED FRESH MINT
- BUTTER, FOR GREASING
- 4 TILAPIA, EACH ABOUT 350 G/12 OZ, SCALED, CLEANED AND BONED
- 55 G/2 OZ PISTACHIO NUTS, FINELY CHOPPED
- SALT AND PEPPER
- 2 TBSP LEMON JUICE
- FRESH MINT SPRIGS, TO GARNISH

1 Heat half the oil in a saucepan. Add the onion and cook over a low heat, stirring occasionally, for 5 minutes, until softened. Add the garlic and cook, stirring for a further 2 minutes. Pour in the fish stock and stir in the couscous and mint. Bring to the boil, then remove the pan from the heat and set aside for 15 minutes, until all the liquid has been absorbed.

2 Meanwhile, preheat the oven to 200°C/400°F/Gas Mark 6. Grease an ovenproof dish, large enough to hold all the fish, with butter.

3 Season the fish inside and out with salt and pepper. Fluff up the couscous mixture with a fork and stir in the nuts, then divide it between the cavities of the fish. Place the fish in the prepared dish and drizzle with the remaining olive oil.

4 Bake for 20 minutes, until the flesh flakes easily. Transfer the fish to warmed serving plates, sprinkle with the lemon juice, garnish with mint sprigs and serve immediately.

GRILLED MUSHROOM & SPINACH-STUFFED TROUT

SERVES 2

INGREDIENTS

- 2 WHOLE TROUT, ABOUT 350 G/12 OZ EACH, GUTTED
- 1 TBSP VEGETABLE OIL
- SALT AND PEPPER

STUFFING

- 25 G/1 OZ BUTTER
- 2 SHALLOTS, FINELY CHOPPED
- 55 G/2 OZ MUSHROOMS, FINELY CHOPPED
- 55 G/2 OZ BABY SPINACH
- 1 TBSP CHOPPED FRESH PARSLEY OR TARRAGON
- GRATED RIND OF 1 LEMON
- WHOLE NUTMEG, FOR GRATING

TOMATO SALSA

- 2 TOMATOES, PEELED, DESEEDED AND FINELY DICED
- 10-CM/4-INCH PIECE OF CUCUMBER, FINELY DICED
- 2 SPRING ONIONS, FINELY CHOPPED
- 1 TBSP OLIVE OIL
- SALT AND PEPPER

1 Clean the trout, trim the fins with a pair of scissors and wipe the inside of the fish with kitchen paper. Leave the head and tail on and slash the skin of each fish on both sides about 5 times. Brush with the oil and season well with salt and pepper, both inside and out.

2 To make the stuffing, melt the butter in a small saucepan and gently soften the shallots for 2–3 minutes. Add the mushrooms and continue to cook for a further 2 minutes. Add the spinach and heat until it is just wilted.

3 Remove from the heat and add the herbs, lemon rind and a good grating of nutmeg. Allow to cool.

4 Fill the trout with the mushroom and spinach stuffing, then reshape them as neatly as you can.

5 Grill the trout under a medium grill for 10–12 minutes, turning once. The skin should be brown and crispy. Alternatively, barbecue for 6–8 minutes on each side, depending on the heat.

6 To make the tomato salsa, mix all the ingredients together and season well with the salt and pepper.

7 Serve the trout hot, with the tomato salsa spooned over them.

TILAPIA WITH
WATERCRESS SAUCE

SERVES 4

INGREDIENTS

- 4 TILAPIA FILLETS, EACH ABOUT
  175 G/6 OZ, SKINNED
- JUICE OF ½ LEMON
- 5 TBSP OLIVE OIL
- 1 SHALLOT, FINELY CHOPPED
- 1 GARLIC CLOVE, FINELY
  CHOPPED
- 115 G/4 OZ WATERCRESS, FINELY
  CHOPPED
- 250 ML/9 FL OZ CRÈME FRAÎCHE
- SALT AND PEPPER
- WATERCRESS SPRIGS,
  TO GARNISH
- NEW POTATOES, TO SERVE

1 Sprinkle the fish fillets with the lemon juice and season with salt and pepper. Heat 3 tablespoons of the olive oil in a frying pan. Add the fish and cook over a medium–low heat for 3–4 minutes on each side.

2 Meanwhile, heat the remaining oil in a saucepan. Add the shallot and garlic and cook over a low heat, stirring occasionally, for 5 minutes, until soft. Stir in the watercress and cook, stirring occasionally, for 2 minutes, until wilted. Stir in the crème fraîche, season to taste with salt and pepper and heat gently.

3 Using a fish slice, transfer the fish fillets to warmed serving plates. Spoon the sauce over them, garnish with the watercress sprigs and serve immediately with the new potatoes.

BAKED CATFISH

SERVES 4

INGREDIENTS

- BUTTER, FOR GREASING
- 115 G/4 OZ UNSALTED PEANUTS, FINELY GROUND
- 4 TBSP SOURED CREAM
- 2 TBSP MILK
- 4 TBSP WHOLEGRAIN MUSTARD
- 4 SPRING ONIONS, FINELY CHOPPED
- 4 CATFISH OR ROCKFISH FILLETS, EACH ABOUT 175 G/ 6 OZ, SKINNED
- LIME WEDGES, TO GARNISH

1 Preheat the oven to 230°C/450°F/Gas Mark 8. Generously grease a baking tray. Spread out the ground peanuts in a shallow dish.

2 Mix together the soured cream, milk, mustard and spring onions in a bowl. Dip the fish fillets in the mixture to coat. You may need to do this more than once to ensure that they are completely covered. Gently roll the fish fillets in the ground peanuts to coat.

3 Place the fish on the prepared baking tray and bake for 8–10 minutes, until the fish flakes easily. Serve immediately, garnished with the lime wedges.

TROUT WITH DRIED FRUIT SAUCE

SERVES 6

INGREDIENTS

- 2 ONIONS, SLICED
- 1 GARLIC CLOVE, FINELY CHOPPED
- 2 CELERY STICKS, SLICED
- 1 CARROT, CHOPPED
- 1 TSP GROUND CUMIN
- 1 TSP GROUND ALLSPICE
- 1 BAY LEAF
- 6 CLOVES
- 6 BLACK PEPPERCORNS
- 225 ML/8 FL OZ WHITE WINE VINEGAR
- 125 ML/4 FL OZ BEER
- 6 TROUT OR CARP STEAKS OR CUTLETS, EACH 175–225 G/ 6–8 OZ
- 25 G/1 OZ BUTTER
- 175 G/6 OZ READY-TO-EAT PRUNES, CHOPPED
- 55 G/2 OZ RAISINS
- 55 G/2 OZ WALNUTS, FINELY CHOPPED
- 1 TBSP BROWN SUGAR
- GRATED RIND AND JUICE OF 1 LEMON
- SALAD LEAVES AND LIME WEDGES, TO SERVE

1 Put the onions, garlic, celery, carrot, cumin, allspice, bay leaf, cloves and peppercorns in a large saucepan and pour in the vinegar, beer and 850 ml/1½ pints of water. Bring to the boil over a medium heat, then reduce the heat, cover and simmer for 30 minutes.

2 Add the fish to the pan, re-cover and simmer for a further 30 minutes, until the flesh flakes easily.

3 Just before the fish is ready, melt the butter in a saucepan. Stir in the prunes, raisins, walnuts, sugar and lemon rind and juice and simmer gently.

4 Using a fish slice, transfer the fish to a warmed serving dish and keep warm. Strain the cooking liquid and discard the vegetables. Measure 450 ml/15 fl oz of the cooking liquid and stir it into the prune and raisin mixture. Cook over a low heat, stirring frequently, for 5 minutes, until heated through. Spoon the sauce over the fish and serve immediately with the salad leaves and lime wedges.

CATFISH **GRATIN**

SERVES 4

INGREDIENTS

- 25 G/1 OZ BUTTER, PLUS EXTRA FOR GREASING
- 1 TBSP SUNFLOWER OIL
- 3 BACON RASHERS, DICED
- 1 ONION, SLICED
- 1 GARLIC CLOVE, FINELY CHOPPED
- 2 RED PEPPERS, DESEEDED AND SLICED
- 400 G/14 OZ CANNED CHOPPED TOMATOES
- 1 TBSP TOMATO PURÉE
- 4 CANNED ANCHOVY FILLETS, DRAINED AND CHOPPED
- DASH OF TABASCO SAUCE
- 4 CATFISH FILLETS, EACH ABOUT 175 G/6 OZ, SKINNED
- 40 G/1½ OZ CHEDDAR CHEESE, GRATED
- 4 TBSP BREADCRUMBS
- SALT AND PEPPER
- COOKED FRENCH BEANS, TO SERVE

1 Preheat the oven to 220°C/425°F/Gas Mark 7. Grease an ovenproof dish with butter.

2 Heat the oil in a saucepan. Add the bacon and cook over a low heat for 2–3 minutes, then add the onion and cook, stirring occasionally, for a further 5 minutes, until soft. Stir in the garlic, peppers, tomatoes, tomato purée, anchovy fillets and Tabasco sauce. Season to taste with salt and pepper, cover and simmer, stirring occasionally, for 15 minutes. Uncover the pan and simmer for a further 5 minutes, until slightly thickened.

3 Place the fish fillets in the prepared dish, season with salt and pepper and dot with the butter. Spoon the sauce over them, place in the preheated oven and bake for 10 minutes.

4 Mix together the cheese and breadcrumbs in a bowl. Remove the fish from the oven and sprinkle the cheese mixture over the top. Return to the oven and bake for a further 10 minutes, until golden brown. Serve immediately, accompanied by the French beans.

SHELLFISH

Once considered a luxurious treat, large stocks of farmed shellfish mean that they are now much more affordable, which is a real bonus for busy cooks. Oysters and clams can be enjoyed raw, but the hallmark of successful shellfish dishes is simple, quick cooking – take care not to overcook or the texture becomes tough. If the idea of Lobster Cooked Beach Style seems too challenging, start off with the familiar Prawn Cocktail.

THE SHELLFISH DIRECTORY

The following is a guide to all the main species of edible shellfish, listed by their common names, although some are known by a variety of different names. The potted profile for each fish details the various forms in which it can be purchased, for example live or cooked, fresh or canned, frozen or smoked, and the most suitable cooking methods.

CLAM

There are many varieties of clam, which vary in size and have either soft or hard shells. They are sold live in their shells and larger clams are steamed open, whereas smaller varieties can be eaten raw. They are also sold smoked and canned.

MUSSEL

Identified by their dark blue shell, mussels cling to rocks or the sea bed and take about two years to reach maturity. They are available live or frozen and are cooked by steaming, which opens their shells. The best known mussels recipe is Moules Marinière.

OYSTER

There are many varieties of this shellfish, which vary in size. The traditional way of eating them is raw, straight from the half shell, with their juices. Shucked (shelled) oysters are available smoked, canned and dried.

SCALLOP AND QUEEN

Scallops and queens both have ribbed fan shells, but queen scallops, or queenies, are smaller than scallops and are more widely available. Unlike other molluscs, scallops cannot hold their shells tightly closed and die soon after they are taken out of water. This means that they are very perishable and are often removed from their shells and iced aboard fishing boats as soon as they are caught. Both the white muscle and orange coral, or roe, are eaten and

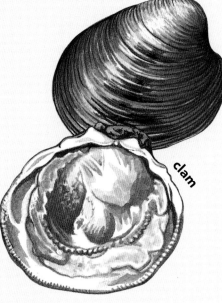

clam

have an exquisite, delicate taste. They can be bought fresh or frozen and can be fried, grilled or steamed.

SHRIMP

This is the smallest crustacean, of which there are several varieties, such as the brown, pink and deep-water shrimp. Like prawns, they are translucent when alive and turn pink when cooked. Shrimps are mainly sold frozen, but are also available canned, salted and dried.

PRAWN

This shellfish is larger than the shrimp and is also available cooked whole or peeled and frozen, canned or dried. A classic way of serving prawns as a starter is Prawn Cocktail.

prawn

scallop

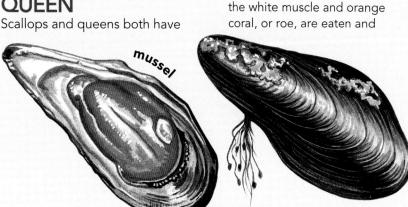

mussel

crab

LOBSTER

Lobster, considered by some to be the finest crustacean, can take seven years to reach marketable size. There are several varieties and they can be bought live, when dark blue, or cooked in the shell, when the lobster turns bright pink. Lobster can also be purchased frozen whole or as frozen tails, and canned. It can be baked, boiled, steamed or grilled.

DUBLIN BAY PRAWN/ LANGOUSTINE/ NORWAY LOBSTER/ SCAMPI

This attractive shellfish looks like a miniature version of a lobster. It is available live or cooked, with its shell or peeled. When peeled and coated in breadcrumbs, it is known as scampi.

ROCK LOBSTER/ SPINY LOBSTER

This is another shellfish that looks similar to a small lobster. It is prepared and cooked in the same way as lobster.

FRESHWATER CRAYFISH

Also resembling a tiny lobster, these are the only shellfish found in fresh waters.

OCTOPUS

The octopus is a cephalopod and has eight tentacles. It varies in size and large ones – as large as 3 metres/10 feet – are available prepared in pieces and small ones are available whole. Octopus can be poached or used in soups and stews.

SQUID

The squid, of which there are several varieties varying in size, is a cephalopod and has ten tentacles. The tentacles are chopped and the body either sliced or kept whole and stuffed. Large squid are usually stewed and small squid can be fried, grilled or poached. The ink, found in a sac, can also be used in cooking. Squid is available fresh or frozen.

CRAB

There are several varieties of this crustacean, including the blue or soft-shell crab, the common crab, the green or shore crab and the spider crab. Crab can be bought live, uncooked in the shell, cooked, with or without the shell, fresh and canned. Its flesh consists of white meat, found in the claws and legs, and brown meat, found in the body. Crab can be baked, steamed or boiled. Fresh crab can also be purchased 'dressed', with the meat arranged attractively in the shell ready for eating. Canned dressed crab is also available.

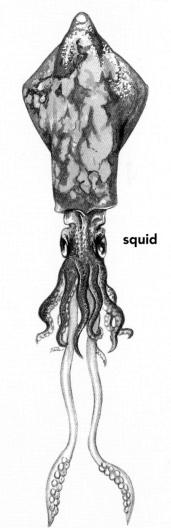

squid

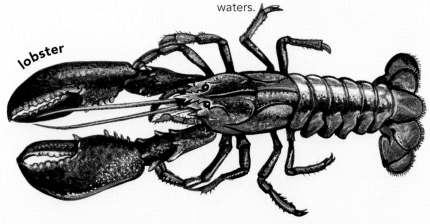

lobster

PREPARING CEPHALOPODS

Although it may seem a bit daunting, there is no great mystery about cleaning and gutting cephalopods, although great care must be taken not to pierce the ink sacs. The step-by-step procedure described below will help to demystify the process.

Squid

Put the squid on a chopping board and, grasping the body in one hand, gently pull off the head and tentacles with the other hand. The body entrails will come away at the same time and should be discarded.

Octopus

Put the octopus on a chopping board and, grasping the body in one hand, firmly pull off the head and tentacles with the other hand. The body entrails will come away at the same time and should be discarded along with the ink sac. Cut off the edible tentacles just in front of the eyes. Rinse the body and tentacles under cold running water and dry on kitchen paper, then beat well with a rolling pin or wooden meat mallet to tenderize the flesh.

SQUID WITH PARSLEY & PINE KERNELS (SEE PAGE 181)

1 Cut off the edible tentacles just in front of the eyes and reserve, then squeeze out the small hard beak and discard.

2 Remove the transparent quill that runs along the length of the body of the squid.

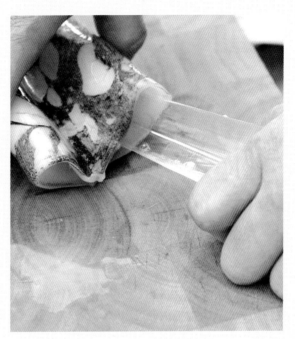

3 Carefully remove one or two of the ink sacs from the head so that you do not pierce them, and reserve them if you want to use the ink in another recipe. Discard the head.

4 Rub off the thin, dark, outer membrane with your fingers. Rinse under cold running water and dry on kitchen paper.

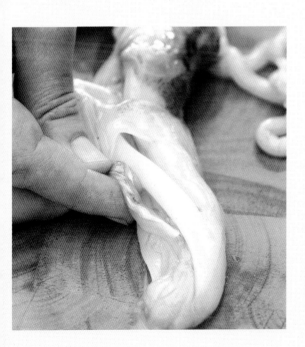

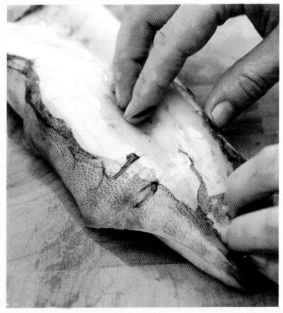

PREPARING SHELLFISH

Buying live shellfish and preparing them at home yourself is actually quite simple if you follow the steps described below. Doing your own preparation will also ensure that when the fish reaches your table it is as fresh as possible.

Crab

Crab is usually sold cooked, but should you buy a live one, the most humane and least traumatic way of killing it is by the following method. Put the live crab in a polythene bag in the freezer for 2 hours to put it to sleep. Bring a large saucepan of heavily salted water to the boil, adding 100 g/3½ oz salt to every 1 litre/1¾ pints. Remove the crab from the freezer, immediately plunge the unconscious crab into the water and cover the saucepan. Return to the boil and simmer for 15 minutes, allowing an extra 10 minutes for each additional crab. Leave the crab to cool in the water.

1 To prepare a cooked crab, have 2 bowls ready, one for white meat and one for brown meat. Put the crab on its back on a chopping board. Gripping a claw firmly in one hand and as close to the body as possible, twist it off. Remove the other claw and the legs in the same way.

2 Break the claws in half by bending them backwards at the joint. Crack the shells of the claws and larger legs with a rolling pin and remove the white meat with a skewer or teaspoon handle. Reserve the small legs for garnishing.

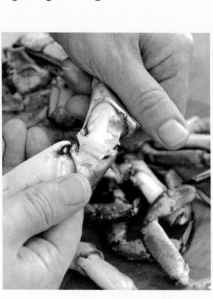

3 Put the crab on its back with its eyes and mouth facing away from you. Remove the stomach sac and mouth, which are attached to the back shell, and discard them.

4 Gripping the shell firmly, press the body section upwards and gently pull them apart. Remove the soft grey gills that are attached along the edges of the body and discard.

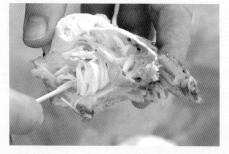

5 Cut the body into 2 or 4 pieces and carefully pick out the flesh. Scoop out the brown meat from the shell.

Lobster

A live lobster should be cooked in the same way as a crab (see page 148), but when you remove it from the freezer, weigh it quickly before plunging it into the water. Calculate the cooking time by allowing 18 minutes for the first 500 g/1 lb 2 oz and an extra 11 minutes for every additional 500 g/1 lb 2 oz.

1 To prepare a cooked lobster, put it on a chopping board and twist off the claws and pincers. Crack open the large claws and remove the flesh, discarding the membrane. The small claws can be reserved for garnishing.

2 Using the point of a sharp knife, split the shell of the lobster in half from head to tail.

4 Remove and discard the thread-like intestine, the stomach sac and the spongy gills.

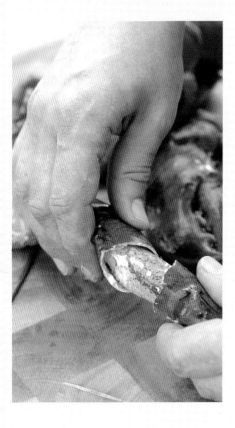

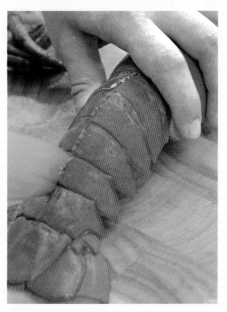

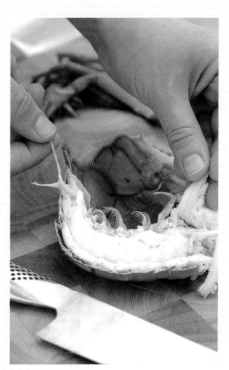

3 Remove the flesh from the tail, reserving the coral (only found in females and at certain times of the year), and, using a skewer, scrape out the flesh from the back legs.

Prawns

1 To peel a prawn, hold its head between your thumb and forefinger and, using the fingers of your other hand, hold the tail and gently pinch and pull off the tail shell.

2 Holding the body, pull off the head, body shell and claws.

3 To devein a prawn, using the point of a sharp knife or skewer, carefully pull out the dark vein that runs down the prawn's back and discard.

Oysters

Scrub each oyster shell with a stiff scrubbing brush under cold running water to clean. To open (shuck) an oyster, put it on a chopping board with the rounded side down, and cover with a clean tea towel to protect your hands.

2 Slide the knife along the inside of the upper shell to cut the muscle and release the oyster. Try to reserve as much of the juice as possible. Oysters served raw 'on the half shell' are served with their juices in the bottom shell.

1 Holding the oyster in the cloth and using a strong, short knife or, ideally, a shucking knife, insert the knife at the hinge and prise the shell upwards to open the oyster shell. Take great care when doing this.

Clams

Scrub each clam with a stiff scrubbing brush under cold running water to clean the shell, then put on a chopping board or hold each clam in a cloth in the palm of your hand and prise the shell open at the hinge with a knife, ideally a clam knife. If the clams are very difficult to open, they can be helped by putting them on a baking tray in a very hot oven for 4–5 minutes until they begin to open.

Loosen the clams and leave each in one half of the shell if you are intending to serve them raw. Reserve any juice from the clams, as this can be strained and used in a sauce. It should certainly not be discarded.

Scallops

1 Scrub each scallop shell with a stiff scrubbing brush under cold running water to remove as much sand as possible.

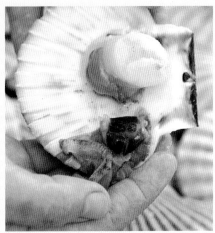

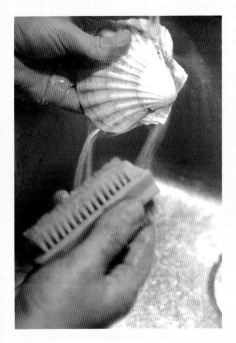

3 Remove and discard the grey beard that surrounds each scallop and the black thread and stomach bag. Detach the scallop and coral from the shell with a spoon. Rinse under cold running water and dry on kitchen paper.

2 Discard any scallops that are open and will not close when tapped sharply with the back of a knife. Using a strong knife, prise the shell open. If the scallops are very difficult to open, they can be helped by putting them on a baking tray, rounded side uppermost, in a very hot oven for 4–5 minutes, until the shells begin to open.

Mussels

Clean each mussel by scrubbing or scraping the shell under cold running water to remove any barnacles, mud or seaweed.

Pull away any beards that are attached to the mussel shells. It is the beard that the mussel uses to cling to the rocks so you will need to tug hard. If the mussel is open and will not close when tapped sharply with the back of a knife, it is dead and should be discarded.

Also discard any with broken shells or any that feel particularly heavy, as these are probably filled with sand. Put the mussels in a colander, rinse well under cold running water, then drain well.

SEAFOOD & BASIL SOUP

SERVES 4

INGREDIENTS

- 2 TBSP VEGETABLE OR GROUNDNUT OIL
- 4 SHALLOTS, FINELY CHOPPED
- 2 GARLIC CLOVES, CHOPPED
- 2 TSP GROUND TURMERIC
- 2 LEMON GRASS STALKS, SNAPPED INTO THREE PIECES
- 2 FRESH GREEN CHILLIES, DESEEDED AND SLICED
- 3 CORIANDER SPRIGS, CHOPPED
- 3 LARGE TOMATOES, PEELED, DESEEDED AND CHOPPED, OR 400 G/14 OZ CANNED TOMATOES, CHOPPED
- 850 ML/1½ PINTS FISH STOCK
- 2 TSP PALM SUGAR OR SOFT, LIGHT BROWN SUGAR
- 2 TBSP FISH SAUCE
- 225 G/8 OZ LIVE MUSSELS
- 12 UNCOOKED KING PRAWNS, PEELED, WITH TAILS LEFT INTACT
- 225 G/8 OZ WHITE FISH FILLET, SKINNED AND CUT INTO LARGE CUBES
- 225 G/8 OZ SQUID, CUT INTO RINGS
- JUICE OF 1 LIME
- 3–4 SPRIGS FRESH THAI BASIL, TO GARNISH

1 Heat the oil in a wok or large frying pan and stir-fry the shallots, garlic, turmeric, lemon grass, chillies and coriander for 1–2 minutes to release the flavours.

2 Add the chopped tomatoes, stock, sugar and fish sauce and simmer for 8–10 minutes.

3 Scrub the mussels under cold running water and tug off the beards. Discard any with broken or damaged shells and those that do not shut immediately when sharply tapped.

4 Add the prawns, mussels, white fish cubes and squid to the wok, cover and simmer for 3–5 minutes, until the fish is cooked and the mussels have opened. Discard any mussels that remain closed. Stir in the lime juice, ladle into warmed bowls, garnish with the Thai basil leaves and serve immediately.

PRAWN COCKTAIL

SERVES 4

INGREDIENTS

- ½ WEBBS LETTUCE, FINELY SHREDDED
- 150 ML/5 FL OZ MAYONNAISE
- 2 TBSP SINGLE CREAM
- 2 TBSP TOMATO KETCHUP
- FEW DROPS OF TABASCO SAUCE, OR TO TASTE
- JUICE OF ½ LEMON, OR TO TASTE
- 175 G/6 OZ COOKED PEELED PRAWNS
- SALT AND PEPPER
- THINLY SLICED BUTTERED BROWN BREAD, TO SERVE (OPTIONAL)

TO GARNISH

- PAPRIKA, FOR SPRINKLING
- 4 COOKED PRAWNS, IN THEIR SHELLS
- 4 LEMON SLICES

1 Divide the lettuce between 4 small serving dishes (traditionally, stemmed glass ones, but any small dishes will be fine).

2 Mix the mayonnaise, cream and tomato ketchup together in a bowl. Add the Tabasco sauce and lemon juice and season well with salt and pepper.

3 Divide the prawns equally between the dishes and pour over the dressing. Cover and leave to chill in the refrigerator for 30 minutes.

4 Sprinkle a little paprika over the cocktails and garnish each dish with a prawn and a lemon slice. Serve the cocktails with the brown bread, if using.

WOK-FRIED KING
PRAWNS IN SPICY SAUCE

SERVES 4

INGREDIENTS

- 3 TBSP VEGETABLE OR GROUNDNUT OIL
- 450 G/1 LB RAW KING PRAWNS, UNPEELED
- 2 TSP FINELY CHOPPED FRESH GINGER
- 1 TSP FINELY CHOPPED GARLIC
- 1 TBSP CHOPPED SPRING ONION
- 2 TBSP CHILLI BEAN SAUCE
- 1 TSP SHAOXING RICE WINE
- 1 TSP SUGAR
- ½ TSP LIGHT SOY SAUCE
- 1–2 TBSP CHICKEN STOCK

1 In a preheated wok or deep saucepan, heat the oil, toss in the prawns and stir-fry over a high heat for about 4 minutes. Arrange the prawns on the sides of the wok, out of the oil, then add the ginger and garlic and stir until fragrant. Add the spring onion and chilli bean sauce. Stir the prawns into the mixture.

2 Reduce the heat slightly and add the rice wine, sugar, soy sauce and stock. Cover and cook for a further minute. Serve immediately.

SCALLOPS WITH BREADCRUMBS & PARSLEY

SERVES 4

INGREDIENTS

- 20 LARGE FRESH SCALLOPS, ABOUT 4 CM/1½ INCHES THICK, REMOVED FROM THEIR SHELLS
- 200 G/7 OZ CLARIFIED BUTTER
- 85 G/3 OZ DAY-OLD FRENCH BREAD, MADE INTO FINE BREADCRUMBS
- 5 TBSP FINELY CHOPPED FRESH FLAT-LEAF PARSLEY
- SALT AND PEPPER
- LEMON WEDGES, TO SERVE (OPTIONAL)

1 Preheat the oven to its lowest temperature. Use a small knife to remove the dark vein that runs around each scallop, then rinse and pat dry. Season to taste with salt and pepper and set aside.

2 Melt half the butter in a large sauté or frying pan over a high heat. Add the breadcrumbs, reduce the heat to medium and fry, stirring, for 5–6 minutes, or until they are golden brown and crisp. Remove the breadcrumbs from the pan, drain well on kitchen paper, then keep warm in the oven. Wipe out the pan.

3 Use 2 large sauté or frying pans to cook all the scallops at once without overcrowding the pans. Melt 50 g/1¾ oz of the butter in each pan over a high heat. Reduce the heat to medium, divide the scallops between the 2 pans in single layers and fry for 2 minutes.

4 Turn the scallops over and fry for a further 2–3 minutes, or until they are golden and cooked through – cut one with a knife to check. Add extra butter to the pans if necessary.

5 Mix the breadcrumbs and parsley together, divide the scallops between 4 warmed plates and sprinkle with the breadcrumbs and parsley mixture. Serve with lemon wedges for squeezing over, if using.

CLAMS IN BLACK BEAN SAUCE

SERVES 2

INGREDIENTS

- 900 G/2 LB SMALL CLAMS
- 1 TBSP VEGETABLE OR GROUNDNUT OIL
- 1 TSP FINELY CHOPPED FRESH GINGER
- 1 TSP FINELY CHOPPED GARLIC
- 1 TBSP FERMENTED BLACK BEANS, RINSED AND ROUGHLY CHOPPED
- 2 TSP SHAOXING RICE WINE
- 1 TBSP FINELY CHOPPED SPRING ONION
- 1 TSP SALT (OPTIONAL)

1 Wash the clams thoroughly, leave to soak in clean water until you are ready to use them, then add to the wok.

2 In a preheated wok or deep saucepan, heat the oil and stir-fry the ginger and garlic until fragrant. Add the black beans and cook for 1 minute.

3 Over a high heat, add the clams and rice wine and stir-fry for 2 minutes to combine all the ingredients. Cover and cook for about 3 minutes. Add the spring onion and the salt, if using, and serve immediately.

STIR-FRIED FRESH CRAB
WITH GINGER

SERVES 4

INGREDIENTS

- 3 TBSP VEGETABLE OR GROUNDNUT OIL
- 2 LARGE FRESH CRABS, CLEANED, BROKEN INTO PIECES, AND LEGS CRACKED WITH A CLEAVER
- 55 G/2 OZ FRESH GINGER, CUT INTO JULIENNE STRIPS
- 100 G/3½ OZ SPRING ONIONS, CHOPPED INTO 5-CM/2-INCH LENGTHS
- 2 TBSP LIGHT SOY SAUCE
- 1 TSP SUGAR
- PINCH OF WHITE PEPPER

1 In a preheated wok or deep saucepan, heat 2 tablespoons of the oil and fry the crab over a high heat for 3–4 minutes. Remove from the wok and set aside.

2 In a clean wok or deep saucepan, heat the remaining oil, add the ginger and stir until fragrant. Add the spring onion, then stir in the crab pieces. Add the soy sauce, sugar and pepper. Cover and simmer for 1 minute and serve immediately.

MOULES MARINIÈRE

SERVES 4

INGREDIENTS

- 300 ML/10 FL OZ DRY WHITE WINE
- 6 SHALLOTS, FINELY CHOPPED
- 1 BOUQUET GARNI
- 2 KG/4 LB 8 OZ LIVE MUSSELS, CLEANED
- PEPPER
- SPRIGS OF FRESH FLAT-LEAF PARSLEY, TO GARNISH
- CRUSTY BREAD, TO SERVE

1 Pour the wine into a large, heavy-based saucepan, add the shallots and bouquet garni and season to taste with pepper. Bring to the boil over a medium heat, add the mussels, cover tightly and cook, shaking the saucepan occasionally, for 3–4 minutes, or until the mussels have opened. Remove and discard the bouquet garni and any mussels that remain closed.

2 Divide the mussels between 4 soup bowls, using a slotted spoon. Tilt the saucepan to let any sand settle, then spoon the cooking liquid over the mussels, garnish with the parsley and serve immediately with the bread.

CARIBBEAN CRAB CAKES

MAKES 16

INGREDIENTS

- 1 POTATO, PEELED AND CUT INTO CHUNKS
- PINCH OF SALT
- 4 SPRING ONIONS, CHOPPED
- 1 GARLIC CLOVE, CHOPPED
- 1 TBSP CHOPPED FRESH THYME
- 1 TBSP CHOPPED FRESH BASIL
- 1 TBSP CHOPPED FRESH CORIANDER
- 225 G/8 OZ WHITE CRABMEAT, DRAINED, IF CANNED, AND THAWED, IF FROZEN
- ½ TSP DIJON MUSTARD
- ½ FRESH GREEN CHILLI, DESEEDED AND FINELY CHOPPED
- 1 EGG, LIGHTLY BEATEN
- PLAIN FLOUR, FOR DUSTING
- SUNFLOWER OIL, FOR SHALLOW-FRYING
- PEPPER
- LIME WEDGES, TO GARNISH
- SALSA OF YOUR CHOICE, TO SERVE

1 Put the potato in a small saucepan, add water to cover and the salt. Bring to the boil, then reduce the heat, cover and simmer for 10–15 minutes until soft. Drain well, turn into a large bowl and mash with a potato masher or fork until smooth.

2 Meanwhile, put the spring onions, garlic, thyme, basil and coriander in a mortar and pound with a pestle until smooth. Add the herb paste to the mashed potato with the crabmeat, mustard, chilli, egg and pepper to taste. Mix well, cover with clingfilm and chill in the refrigerator for 30 minutes.

3 Sprinkle flour onto a large, flat plate. Shape spoonfuls of the crabmeat mixture into small balls with your hands, then flatten slightly and dust with flour, shaking off any excess. Heat the oil in a frying pan over a high heat, add the crab cakes and cook in batches for 2–3 minutes on each side until golden. Remove with a slotted spoon and drain on kitchen paper. Set aside to cool to room temperature.

4 Arrange the crab cakes on a serving dish, garnish with the lime wedges and serve with a bowl of salsa.

GOAT'S CHEESE &
OYSTER TARTLETS

MAKES 12

INGREDIENTS

- 125 G/4½ OZ PLAIN FLOUR, PLUS EXTRA FOR DUSTING
- PINCH OF SALT
- 100 G/3½ OZ BUTTER, DICED, PLUS EXTRA FOR GREASING
- 1 EGG YOLK
- 1 ONION, CHOPPED
- 12 LIVE OYSTERS, SHUCKED
- 2 TBSP CHOPPED FRESH FLAT-LEAF PARSLEY, PLUS EXTRA SPRIGS TO GARNISH
- SALT AND PEPPER
- 200 G/7 OZ GOAT'S CHEESE, CRUMBLED

1 Grease twelve 7-cm/2¾-inch tartlet tins. Sift the flour and salt together into a bowl. Rub 90 g/3¼ oz of the butter into the flour until fine crumbs form. Mix in the egg yolk to make a dough. Add a little cold water if needed. Shape into a ball and turn out onto a lightly floured work surface. Roll out to a thickness of 5 mm/¼ inch. Line the prepared tins with the pastry and trim the edges. Cover and chill in the refrigerator for 45 minutes.

2 Preheat the oven to 200°C/400°F/Gas Mark 6. Remove the tartlet cases from the refrigerator and bake in the preheated oven for 10 minutes until golden.

3 Meanwhile, heat the remaining butter in a saucepan over a medium heat, add the onion and cook, stirring frequently for 4 minutes. Add the oysters, parsley, and salt and pepper to taste, and cook, stirring, for 1 minute.

4 Remove the tartlet cases from the oven. Divide half of the goat's cheese between them. Top with the oyster mixture, sprinkle over the remaining cheese, then bake for a further 10 minutes. Garnish the tartlets with the parsley sprigs and serve hot.

CALAMARES

SERVES 6

INGREDIENTS

- 450 G/1 LB PREPARED SQUID
- PLAIN FLOUR, FOR COATING
- SUNFLOWER OIL, FOR DEEP-FRYING
- SALT
- LEMON WEDGES, TO GARNISH
- AÏOLI, TO SERVE (SEE PAGE 24)

1 Slice the squid into 1-cm/½-inch rings and halve the tentacles if large. Rinse under cold running water and dry well with kitchen paper. Dust the squid rings with flour so that they are lightly coated.

2 Heat the oil in a deep-fat fryer, large, heavy-based saucepan or wok to 180°C/350°F, or until a cube of bread browns in 30 seconds. Fry the squid rings in small batches for 2–3 minutes, or until golden brown and crisp all over, turning several times (if you fry too many squid rings at once, the oil temperature will drop and the rings will be soggy). Do not overcook as the squid will become tough and rubbery rather than moist and tender.

3 Remove with a slotted spoon and drain well on kitchen paper. Keep warm in a low oven while you fry the remaining squid rings.

4 Sprinkle the fried squid rings with salt and serve piping hot, garnished with lemon wedges for squeezing over. Accompany with a bowl of Aïoli for dipping.

SEAFOOD PASTA PARCELS

SERVES 4

INGREDIENTS

- 1.5 KG/3 LB 5 OZ FRESHLY COOKED CRABMEAT, SHELLS RESERVED
- 2 TBSP VIRGIN OLIVE OIL
- 2 FRESH RED CHILLIES, DESEEDED AND FINELY CHOPPED
- 4 GARLIC CLOVES, FINELY CHOPPED
- 800 G/1 LB 12 OZ CANNED TOMATOES
- 225 ML/8 FL OZ DRY WHITE WINE
- 350 G/12 OZ DRIED SPAGHETTI
- 2 TBSP BUTTER
- 115 G/4 OZ PREPARED SQUID, SLICED
- 175 G/6 OZ RAW MEDITERRANEAN PRAWNS
- 450 G/1 LB LIVE MUSSELS, CLEANED
- 3 TBSP COARSELY CHOPPED FRESH FLAT-LEAF PARSLEY
- 1 TBSP SHREDDED FRESH BASIL LEAVES, PLUS EXTRA SPRIGS TO GARNISH
- SALT AND PEPPER

1 Carefully break up the larger pieces of crab shell with a meat mallet or the end of a rolling pin.

2 Heat 1 tablespoon of the olive oil in a large saucepan. Add half the chillies and half the garlic, then add the pieces of crab shell. Cook over a medium heat, stirring occasionally, for 2–3 minutes. Add the tomatoes with their can juices and the wine. Reduce the heat and simmer for about 1 hour.

3 Strain the sauce, pressing down on the contents of the sieve with a wooden spoon. Season to taste with salt and pepper and set aside.

4 Bring a large saucepan of lightly salted water to the boil. Add the pasta, bring back to the boil and cook for 8–10 minutes, until the pasta is tender, but still firm to the bite.

5 Heat the remaining oil with the butter in a large, heavy-based saucepan. Add the remaining chilli and garlic and cook over a low heat, stirring occasionally, for 5 minutes, until soft. Add the squid, prawns and mussels, cover and cook over a high heat for 4–5 minutes, until the mussels have opened. Add the crabmeat and heat through for 2–3 minutes. Remove the saucepan from the heat and discard any mussels that remain closed.

6 Drain the pasta and add it to the seafood with the chilli and tomato sauce, parsley and basil, tossing well to coat.

7 Cut out 4 large squares of baking paper or greaseproof paper. Divide the pasta and seafood between them, placing it on one half. Fold over the other half and turn in the edges securely to seal. Transfer to a large baking tray and bake in a preheated oven, 180°C/350°F/Gas Mark 4, for about 10 minutes, until the parcels have puffed up. Serve immediately, garnished with the basil sprigs.

MUSSELS WITH HERB & GARLIC BUTTER

SERVES 8

INGREDIENTS

- 800 G/1 LB 12 OZ LIVE MUSSELS, CLEANED
- SPLASH OF DRY WHITE WINE
- 1 BAY LEAF
- 85 G/3 OZ BUTTER
- 35 G/1¼ OZ FRESH WHITE OR BROWN BREADCRUMBS
- 4 TBSP CHOPPED FRESH FLAT-LEAF PARSLEY, PLUS EXTRA SPRIGS TO GARNISH
- 2 TBSP SNIPPED FRESH CHIVES
- 2 GARLIC CLOVES, FINELY CHOPPED
- SALT AND PEPPER
- LEMON WEDGES, TO SERVE

1 Preheat the oven to 230°C/450°F/Gas Mark 8.

2 Put the mussels in a large saucepan and add the wine and bay leaf. Cook, covered, over a high heat, shaking the saucepan occasionally, for 3–4 minutes, or until the mussels have opened. Discard any that remain closed. Strain the mussels.

3 Shell the mussels, reserving one half of each shell. Arrange the mussels, in their half shells, in a large, shallow, ovenproof serving dish.

4 Melt the butter in a small saucepan and pour into a small bowl. Add the breadcrumbs, parsley, chives, garlic, and salt and pepper to taste, and mix together well. Leave until the butter has set slightly. Using your fingers or 2 teaspoons, take a large pinch of the butter mixture and use to fill each mussel shell, pressing it down well.

5 Bake the mussels in the preheated oven for 10 minutes, or until hot. Serve immediately, garnished with the parsley sprigs, accompanied by the lemon wedges for squeezing over.

GARLIC & HERB DUBLIN BAY PRAWNS

SERVES 2

INGREDIENTS

- JUICE OF ½ LEMON
- 2 GARLIC CLOVES, CRUSHED
- 3 TBSP CHOPPED FRESH PARSLEY
- 1 TBSP CHOPPED FRESH DILL
- 3 TBSP SOFTENED BUTTER
- 12 RAW DUBLIN BAY PRAWNS
- SALT AND PEPPER
- LEMON WEDGES AND FRESH CRUSTY BREAD, TO SERVE

1 Preheat the grill to medium. Mix the lemon juice with the garlic, herbs and butter to form a paste. Season well with the salt and pepper. Spread the paste over the prawns and leave to marinate for 30 minutes.

2 Cook the prawns under the preheated grill for 5–6 minutes. Alternatively, heat a frying pan and fry the prawns in the paste until cooked. Turn out onto hot plates and pour over the pan juices. Serve at once with the lemon wedges and bread.

LOBSTER THERMIDOR

SERVES 4

INGREDIENTS

- 2 COOKED LOBSTERS, ABOUT 750 G/1 LB 10 OZ EACH
- 55 G/2 OZ BUTTER
- 1 SHALLOT, CHOPPED
- 25 G/1 OZ PLAIN FLOUR
- 300 ML/10 FL OZ MILK
- 1½ TSP CHOPPED FRESH CHERVIL
- 1 TSP CHOPPED FRESH TARRAGON
- 1½ TSP CHOPPED FRESH PARSLEY
- 2 TSP DIJON MUSTARD
- SALT AND PEPPER
- 6 TBSP DRY WHITE WINE
- 3 TBSP DOUBLE CREAM
- 4 TBSP FRESHLY GRATED PARMESAN CHEESE
- LEMON WEDGES AND FRESH PARSLEY SPRIGS, TO GARNISH

1 Preheat the grill to hot. Twist off and discard the lobster heads and pull off the claws. Crack the claws with a small hammer and remove the flesh. Using a sharp knife, split the lobsters in half lengthways and remove and discard the intestinal vein. Remove the flesh and reserve. Scrub the half-shells under cold running water and drain upside down on kitchen paper. Cut the lobster flesh into 2-cm/¾-inch thick slices.

2 Melt the butter in a heavy-based saucepan. Add the shallot and cook over a low heat for 4–5 minutes, or until soft. Sprinkle in the flour and cook, stirring constantly, for 2 minutes. Remove the pan from the heat and gradually stir in the milk. Return the pan to the heat and bring to the boil, stirring. Cook, stirring, until thickened and smooth.

3 Reduce the heat, stir in the herbs and mustard and season to taste with salt and pepper. Remove the saucepan from the heat and whisk in the wine and cream. Return to a low heat and simmer until thickened. Add the lobster flesh and heat through for 2–3 minutes.

4 Divide the mixture between the half-shells and sprinkle with the Parmesan cheese. Cook under the preheated grill until the topping is golden and bubbling. Serve at once, garnished with the lemon wedges and parsley sprigs.

SQUID WITH PARSLEY & PINE KERNELS

SERVES 4

INGREDIENTS

- 85 G/3 OZ SULTANAS
- 5 TBSP OLIVE OIL
- 6 TBSP CHOPPED FRESH FLAT-LEAF PARSLEY, PLUS EXTRA TO GARNISH
- 2 GARLIC CLOVES, FINELY CHOPPED
- 800 G/1 LB 12 OZ PREPARED SQUID, SLICED, OR SQUID RINGS
- 125 ML/4 FL OZ DRY WHITE WINE
- 500 ML/17 FL OZ PASSATA
- PINCH OF CHILLI POWDER
- 85 G/3 OZ PINE KERNELS, FINELY CHOPPED
- SALT

1 Place the sultanas in a small bowl, cover with lukewarm water and set aside for 15 minutes to plump up.

2 Meanwhile, heat the olive oil in a heavy-based saucepan. Add the parsley and garlic and cook over a low heat, stirring frequently, for 3 minutes. Add the squid and cook, stirring occasionally, for 5 minutes.

3 Increase the heat to medium, pour in the wine and cook until it has almost completely evaporated. Stir in the passata and season to taste with chilli powder and salt. Reduce the heat, cover and simmer gently, stirring occasionally, for 45–50 minutes, until the squid is almost tender.

4 Drain the sultanas and stir them into the pan with the pine kernels. Simmer for a further 10 minutes, then serve immediately.

CRAYFISH IN CREAMY TOMATO SAUCE

SERVES 4

INGREDIENTS

- 55 G/2 OZ BUTTER
- 2 SHALLOTS, FINELY CHOPPED
- 4 TOMATOES, PEELED AND CHOPPED
- 2 TBSP TOMATO PURÉE
- PINCH OF DRIED OREGANO
- PINCH OF SUGAR (OPTIONAL)
- 450 G/1 LB PEELED CRAYFISH TAILS
- 4 TBSP DOUBLE CREAM
- SALT AND PEPPER

TO SERVE
- BOILED WILD RICE
- ROCKET LEAVES
- LEMON WEDGES

1 Melt the butter in a saucepan. Add the shallots and cook over a low heat, stirring occasionally, for 5 minutes, until soft. Stir in the tomatoes, tomato purée and oregano, cover and simmer gently for 10–15 minutes, until pulpy. Taste, stir in the sugar if the sauce is too sharp and season with salt and pepper.

2 Stir in the crayfish tails and cream and heat through gently for 2–3 minutes, stirring occasionally. Serve immediately on a bed of wild rice, accompanied by the rocket leaves and lemon wedges.

OCTOPUS WITH LEMON & CHILLI DRESSING

SERVES 4

INGREDIENTS

- 2 KG/4 LB 8 OZ OCTOPUS, CLEANED AND GUTTED
- 350–425 ML/12–15 FL OZ OLIVE OIL
- JUICE AND FINELY GRATED RIND OF 1 LEMON
- 1–2 GREEN CHILLIES, DESEEDED AND FINELY CHOPPED
- 1–2 GARLIC CLOVES, FINELY CHOPPED
- 1 TBSP CHOPPED FRESH CORIANDER
- SALT AND PEPPER
- SALAD LEAVES, TO SERVE

1 Preheat the oven to 150°C/350°F/Gas Mark 2.

2 Place the octopus in a lidded casserole just large enough to hold it and pour in just enough olive oil to cover. Cover and cook in the preheated oven for 2 hours, until very tender.

3 Drain the octopus well and discard the cooking oil. Separate the tentacles and run your hand firmly along each one to remove the suckers. Thinly slice the tentacles and place in a bowl.

4 Mix together 125 ml/4 fl oz of the remaining olive oil, the lemon juice and rind, chillies, garlic and coriander in jug. Season to taste with salt and pepper and pour the dressing over the octopus. Toss gently, then cover with clingfilm and chill in the refrigerator for at least 2 hours. Serve on a bed of salad leaves.

MARINATED SCAMPI

SERVES 4

INGREDIENTS
- 24 PEELED SCAMPI TAILS
- 4 TBSP LEMON JUICE
- 4 TBSP OLIVE OIL, PLUS EXTRA
  FOR BRUSHING
- 2 TSP CHOPPED FRESH MINT
- 2 TSP CHOPPED FRESH PARSLEY
- SALT AND PEPPER
- 24 PROSCIUTTO SLICES
- LIME WEDGES AND SALAD
  LEAVES, TO SERVE

1 Put the scampi in a non-metallic bowl. Mix the lemon juice, olive oil, mint and parsley together in a jug and season with salt and pepper. Pour the mixture over the scampi and toss lightly to coat. Cover with clingfilm and set aside in a cool place to marinate for 1 hour.

2 Line a grill pan with foil and brush with olive oil. Preheat the grill.

3 Drain the scampi, reserving the marinade. Wrap each scampi tail in a slice of prosciutto and secure with a cocktail stick. Spread them out on the grill pan and cook for 10–12 minutes, turning and brushing with the reserved marinade occasionally. Serve immediately with the lime wedges and salad leaves.

OYSTERS WITH A SPICY DRESSING

SERVES 4

INGREDIENTS

- 125 ML/4 FL OZ SUNFLOWER OIL
- 1 TBSP LIGHT SOY SAUCE
- 2 TBSP RICE VINEGAR
- 2 TBSP LIME JUICE
- 1 RED CHILLI, DESEEDED AND FINELY CHOPPED
- 1 GARLIC CLOVE, FINELY CHOPPED
- 1 TBSP FINELY CHOPPED FRESH GINGER
- 2 TSP FINELY CHOPPED FRESH CORIANDER
- 24 LIVE OYSTERS, PREPARED, ON THE HALF SHELL
- THINLY SLICED BROWN BREAD AND BUTTER (OPTIONAL) AND LEMON WEDGES, TO SERVE

1 Mix together the oil, soy sauce, vinegar, lime juice, chilli, garlic, ginger and coriander in a bowl and set aside.

2 One at a time, remove the oysters from the half shells with a slotted spoon and dip them into the dressing. Take care not to spill the natural juices that accumulate in the shells.

3 Return the oysters to the half shells and serve immediately on a bed of ice with some thinly sliced brown bread and butter, if using, and the lemon wedges.

LOBSTER COOKED BEACH STYLE

SERVES 4

INGREDIENTS

- 2–4 COOKED LOBSTERS, DEPENDING ON THEIR SIZE, CUT THROUGH THE MIDDLE INTO TWO HALVES, OR 4 LOBSTER TAILS, THE MEAT LOOSENED SLIGHTLY FROM ITS SHELL

CHILLI BUTTER

- 115 G/4 OZ UNSALTED BUTTER, SOFTENED
- 3–4 TBSP CHOPPED FRESH CORIANDER
- ABOUT 5 GARLIC CLOVES, CHOPPED
- 2–3 TBSP MILD CHILLI POWDER
- JUICE OF 1 LIME
- SALT AND PEPPER

TO SERVE

- SALAD LEAVES
- LIME WEDGES
- SALSA OF YOUR CHOICE

1 Light the barbecue. To make the chilli butter, put the butter in a bowl and mix in the coriander, garlic, chilli powder and lime juice. Add salt and pepper to taste.

2 Rub the chilli butter into the cut side of the lobster or the lobster tails, working it into all the cracks and crevices.

3 Wrap loosely in foil and place, cut side up, on a rack over the hot coals of the barbecue. Cook for 15 minutes, or until heated through.

4 Serve with the salad leaves, lime wedges and salsa.

5

PRESERVED FISH

For generations, skilled cooks have canned, dried, smoked and pickled fish for year-round consumption. Today's modern transportation networks and refrigeration mean such efforts are no longer essential, but preserved fish remains popular because of the outstanding flavours and textures achieved. Preserved fish can be used in recipes as diverse as sushi and Smoked Trout with Pears. And, of course, having canned fish in the cupboard means you can always prepare a meal in a flash.

WAYS TO PRESERVE FISH

In the days before modern refrigeration and transportation fish preservation was necessary to prevent spoilage and ensure year-round supplies. That isn't the case any longer, but canned, dried, frozen, pickled, salted and smoked fish remain popular because of their unique flavours, versatility and convenience.

Cans of goodness

Cans of anchovy fillets, clams, mussels, oysters, salmon, mackerel, shrimp and sardines are handy staples in every kitchen to add flavour to quick sandwich fillings, pasta sauces and baked suppers.

The canning process, which gives fish long shelf lives of several years, preserves many of the seafood's vitamins and minerals, but you should, however, always note the best-before dates.

Canned tuna is available preserved in brine, oil and spring water for variety, and you'll also find sardines canned in tomato sauce and oil.

Dried and salted for long life

Both air-drying and salting are ancient techniques for removing moisture from fresh fish, delaying spoilage for varying lengths of time. One of the most fascinating transformations in the culinary world is how a piece of dried salt cod that looks like dry cardboard is transformed into tender, flaky fish by lengthy soaking in water. Especially popular in Mediterranean and Scandinavian countries, salt cod, also called *stockfish* in Scandinavia, *morue* in France, *baccala* in Italy and *bacalhau* in Portugal, was once an essential winter staple, but today its appeal is its flavour. It remains a popular ingredient in dishes such as fish cakes or creamed salt cod. It is usually sold in long, dried fillets. Try to buy middle slices, as they will cook most evenly.

Caviar is salted sturgeon roe, although less expensive salted lumpfish and salmon roes are also available as are dried cod and grey mullet roes. A dry mixture of salt, peppercorns and dill are rubbed on salmon fillets to make Gravadlax, a Scandinavian favourite.

Frozen or fresh?

Although it might sound like a contradiction in terms, frozen fish is often fresher than the fish you buy at the fishmongers. Large commercial fishing vessels are capable of processing and freezing the catch within hours of it coming

CANNED ANCHOVIES

out of the water, which keeps it in prime condition. If you follow the instructions on the packaging, steaks and fillets can be cooked from frozen.

In a pickle

Pickling is an old-fashioned form of preserving that remains popular because the sweet-sour taste of the flavoured vinegar, or brine, enhances the taste of the fish. Oily fish, because of the natural oils they contain, are well suited to this process. Rollmops, pickled herring rolled around onions and spices, for example, have travelled from Scandinavia to tables around the globe.

In hot climates, such as South America, the Mediterranean and Mexico, fresh white fish and shellfish are left to marinate in lemon or lime juice with herbs for a quick form of pickling that is intended for immediate consumption. The acid in the juice 'cooks' the flesh, making it safe for human consumption.

Simply smoked

Smoked salmon is perhaps the best-known smoked fish, but many other species are also successfully smoked. Oily fish, such as herring and mackerel, are, ideal and haddock, trout and shellfish are also popular. (Cans of smoked mussels and oysters are useful for making impromptu nibbles to enjoy with drinks.)

Scottish smoked haddock, such as finnan haddock and Arbroath smokies, for example, like a myriad of other examples, are enjoyed around the world in soups, rich pâtés and mousses and as breakfast dishes.

SMOKED MACKEREL

Fish is either cold-smoked or hot-smoked. Cold-smoked fish is first brined or salted before being left to hang over a slow-burning fire. Although all producers follow the same basic technique that has been used for generations, they stamp their individual mark on the final product by using different-flavoured brine and different wood chips for the smoke. If possible, always taste before you buy.

Some cold-smoked fish is ready to eat, while others will require cooking. When a fish is hot smoked, however, it is given an initial blast of hot air at the beginning of the process before slow smoking, so it is ready to eat, making it a very healthy type of fast food.

GRAVADLAX

PREPARING SUSHI

Sushi originated centuries ago as a way of extending the shelf life of dried fish by placing it between layers of vinegared rice. The word sushi actually refers to the vinegared rice, but its meaning has now been extended to describe a finger-sized piece of raw fish or seafood on a bed of cold vinegared rice.

Equipment needed
Very little specialized equipment is required, although you can buy sushi-making kits in various outlets, including larger supermarkets. The key to the technique is a bamboo sushi mat with which to make the most common form, rolled sushi. A kit may include a special mixing tub, a pressing box and a spatula.

Which fish?
Meatier types of round fish, such as cod, tuna, salmon, trout, mackerel and eel, are all suitable for sushi, as are prawns, lobster, squid, scallops, crab and fish roe. Smoked versions of haddock, salmon, trout and mackerel are also popular. Many sushi recipes use raw fish. Always buy it from a reliable supplier who offers 'sushi' or 'sashimi grade' fish, which is as fresh as possible, because raw fish contains more bacteria and parasites than cooked fish. Similarly, look for shellfish that come from certified waters. Only buy fish or shellfish on the day you intend to eat it and keep it refrigerated.

Preparing sushi rice
Sushi is a short-grained rice, and several brands are available. The hot cooked rice is tipped into a large, shallow dish and sushi rice seasoning spread over the surface. With one hand you mix in the seasoning with a spatula; with the other you fan the rice to cool it quickly. The finished rice should have a shiny appearance and be at room temperature.

Presenting sushi
Presentation is all, and the best sushi are minor works of culinary art. You need to have all the ingredients assembled, the rice cooled and the garnishes, pickles or dipping sauces prepared so that you can serve the sushi immediately.

Scattered sushi
This is where sushi rice is mixed loosely with other ingredients, and is very easy to make. It is often served as an attractive individual bowl for each person.

Rolled sushi

These are best made using a sushi mat.

A sheet of nori (dried seaweed), is placed on the bamboo mat and the filling heaped along the bottom third of the nori.

By folding the mat over the filling, then lifting the mat and keeping an even pressure along the length, the roll is formed. It is cut, using a very sharp, wet knife, into rounds, which are then turned on one end to present the filling.

Boat sushi

These dishes are prepared by wrapping nori around rice moulded into oval shapes. Using nori is an ideal way to serve sushi with fish roe or soft toppings that would otherwise be messy to handle.

Pressed sushi

This type is made by pressing the rice into a special three-piece bamboo box, although you can improvise using a loose-based tin or terrine tin with drop-down sides. If you have a fixed-base tin, the sushi has to be made upside down, and the sushi turned out after the flavours have had time to mix and develop.

SCATTERED SUSHI WITH
SMOKED MACKEREL

SERVES 4

INGREDIENTS

- 8 MANGETOUT
- 5-CM/2-INCH PIECE MOOLI
- 1 QUANTITY FRESHLY COOKED SUSHI RICE (SEE PAGE 25)
- JUICE AND FINELY GRATED RIND OF 1 LEMON
- 2 SPRING ONIONS, FINELY CHOPPED
- 2 SMOKED MACKEREL FILLETS, SKINNED, CUT INTO DIAGONAL STRIPS
- ½ CUCUMBER, PEELED AND CUT INTO SLICES

TO GARNISH

- PICKLED GINGER
- STRIPS OF TOASTED NORI
- WASABI PASTE

1 Bring a saucepan of lightly salted water to the boil, add the mangetout and blanch for 1 minute. Drain and set aside to cool. Shred the mooli using the finest setting on a mandolin or a very sharp knife. If you are using a knife, cut the mooli into long, thin slices and cut each slice along its length as finely as you can.

2 Mix the rice with the lemon juice and rind.

3 Divide the rice between 4 wooden or ceramic bowls – they should be about 2 cm/¾ inch full. Scatter the spring onions over the top. Arrange the mackerel, cucumber, mangetout and mooli on top of the rice. Garnish with the pickled ginger, nori strips and a small mound of wasabi paste.

PRESSED SUSHI BARS
WITH SMOKED SALMON & CUCUMBER

MAKES 8–10

INGREDIENTS

- VEGETABLE OIL, FOR OILING
- ½ QUANTITY FRESHLY COOKED SUSHI RICE (SEE PAGE 25)
- 2 TBSP JAPANESE MAYONNAISE
- 200 G/7 OZ SMOKED SALMON
- ½ CUCUMBER, PEELED AND CUT INTO VERY THIN SLICES
- LEMON WEDGES AND FRESH MINT SPRIGS, TO GARNISH

1 Oil an oshi waku or terrine tin (preferably with drop-down sides) and line it with a piece of clingfilm so that the clingfilm hangs over the edges. This is to help you lift out the sushi later. Pack the tin 3 cm/1¼ inches full with the rice. Spread a layer of mayonnaise on top of the rice. Arrange the smoked salmon and cucumber in diagonal strips on top of the rice, doubling up the smoked salmon layers if you have enough so that the topping is quite thick. Cover the top of the rice with a strip of clingfilm, put another terrine tin on top of the clingfilm and weigh down with a couple of food cans.

2 Chill the sushi in the refrigerator for 15 minutes. Remove the cans and the top tin, then lift out the sushi. Cut the sushi into 8–10 pieces with a very sharp, wet knife. Garnish with the lemon wedges and mint sprigs before serving.

SUSHI
BOATS

SMOKED TROUT SUSHI BOATS

MAKES 8 PIECES

INGREDIENTS

- ⅓ QUANTITY FRESHLY COOKED SUSHI RICE (SEE PAGE 25)
- 2 SMALL SHEETS OF TOASTED NORI, EACH CUT INTO 4 STRIPS LENGTHWAYS
- 2 TBSP JAPANESE MAYONNAISE
- 1 TSP GRATED LEMON ZEST
- 2 TSP LEMON JUICE
- 2 SPRING ONIONS, FINELY CHOPPED
- 1 SMOKED TROUT FILLET, FLAKED
- 55 G/2 OZ SMOKED SALMON, CUT INTO STRIPS
- PONZU SAUCE AND 4 RADISHES, FINELY CHOPPED, TO SERVE

1 Divide the rice into 8 batches. Dampen your hands to prevent the rice sticking, then shape each batch of the rice into an oval using your hands.

2 Carefully wrap a strip of nori around each piece of rice, trim off any excess, then stick together at the join using a couple of crushed grains of rice.

3 Mix the mayonnaise with the lemon zest and juice and spread a little on top of each sushi boat. Sprinkle with some spring onion, then top with some of the smoked trout and smoked salmon. Serve the sushi straight away with the ponzu sauce and chopped radish.

SMOKED FISH PÂTÉ

SERVES 8

INGREDIENTS

- 900 G/2 LB UNDYED KIPPER FILLETS
- 2 GARLIC CLOVES, FINELY CHOPPED
- 175 ML/6 FL OZ OLIVE OIL
- 6 TBSP SINGLE CREAM
- SALT AND PEPPER
- LEMON SLICES, TO GARNISH
- OATCAKES, TO SERVE

1 Put the kippers in a large frying pan or fish kettle and add cold water to just cover. Bring to the boil, then immediately reduce the heat and poach gently for 10 minutes until tender. If using a frying pan, you may need to do this in batches.

2 Transfer the fish to a chopping board using a fish slice. Remove and discard the skin. Roughly flake the flesh with a fork and remove and discard any remaining tiny bones. Transfer the fish to a saucepan over a low heat, add the garlic and break up the fish with a wooden spoon.

3 Gradually add the oil, beating well after each addition. Add the cream and beat until smooth, but do not allow the mixture to boil.

4 Remove the saucepan from the heat and season to taste with salt, if necessary, and pepper. Spoon the pâté into a serving dish, cover and set aside to cool completely. Chill in the refrigerator until required, for up to 3 days.

5 Garnish with the lemon slices and serve with the oatcakes.

CREAMED SALT COD

SERVES 4–6

INGREDIENTS

- 700 G/1 LB 9 OZ SALT COD
- 300 ML/10 FL OZ OLIVE OIL
- 2 LARGE GARLIC CLOVES, VERY FINELY CHOPPED
- 300 ML/10 FL OZ SINGLE CREAM
- LEMON JUICE, TO TASTE
- PEPPER
- BLACK OLIVES, STONED AND HALVED, AND CHOPPED
- FRESH FLAT-LEAF PARSLEY, TO GARNISH
- FRIED CROÛTES, TO SERVE

1 Cut or break the salt cod into pieces that will fit in a large bowl of water, then leave to soak for up to 48 hours, replacing the water with fresh water about every 8 hours to remove the saltiness.

2 Drain the salt cod, then transfer it to a saucepan and cover with fresh water. Slowly bring to a simmer and leave to simmer for 15–20 minutes until it is tender and flakes easily.

3 Meanwhile, heat the oil in a heavy-based saucepan just until the surface shimmers. Add the garlic and set aside to infuse.

4 Drain the salt cod. When it is cool enough to handle, remove all the skin and small bones, then flake the flesh into a food processor.

5 Reheat the garlic-infused oil and heat the cream in a separate saucepan. With the food processor's motor running, add about 2 tablespoons of the oil, then 2 tablespoons of the cream to the cod. Continue adding the oil and cream until they are absorbed and the cod has the consistency of mashed potatoes.

6 Taste the mixture and add pepper and lemon juice to taste. Extra salt shouldn't be necessary. Mound the salt cod mixture on a serving platter and garnish with the olive halves, then sprinkle parsley over. Serve with the fried croûtes.

TUNA-NOODLE CASSEROLE

SERVES 4–5

INGREDIENTS

- 200 G/7 OZ DRIED RIBBON PASTA, SUCH AS TAGLIATELLE
- 25 G/1 OZ BUTTER
- 55 G/2 OZ FINE FRESH BREADCRUMBS
- 400 ML/14 FL OZ CONDENSED CANNED CREAM OF MUSHROOM SOUP
- 125 ML/4 FL OZ MILK
- 2 CELERY STICKS, CHOPPED
- 1 RED AND 1 GREEN PEPPER, DESEEDED AND CHOPPED
- 140 G/5 OZ MATURE CHEDDAR CHEESE, ROUGHLY GRATED
- 2 TBSP CHOPPED FRESH PARSLEY, PLUS EXTRA SPRIGS TO GARNISH
- 200 G/7 OZ CANNED TUNA IN OIL, DRAINED AND FLAKED
- SALT AND PEPPER

1 Preheat the oven to 200°C/400°F/ Gas Mark 6. Bring a large saucepan of lightly salted water to the boil. Add the pasta and cook for 2 minutes less than specified on the packet instructions.

2 Meanwhile, melt the butter in a small saucepan over a medium heat. Stir in the breadcrumbs, then remove from the heat and reserve.

3 Drain the pasta well and reserve. Pour the soup into the pasta pan over a medium heat, then stir in the milk, celery, peppers, half the cheese and all the parsley. Add the tuna and gently stir in so that the flakes don't break up. Season to taste with salt and pepper. Heat just until small bubbles appear around the edge of the mixture – do not boil.

4 Stir the pasta into the pan and use 2 forks to mix all the ingredients together. Spoon the mixture into an ovenproof dish that is also suitable for serving and spread out.

5 Stir the remaining cheese into the buttered breadcrumbs, then sprinkle over the top of the pasta mixture. Bake in the oven for 20–25 minutes until the topping is golden. Leave to stand for 5 minutes before serving straight from the dish.

BAVETTINE WITH SMOKED SALMON & ROCKET

SERVES 4

INGREDIENTS

- 350 G/12 OZ DRIED BAVETTINE
- 2 TBSP OLIVE OIL
- 1 GARLIC CLOVE, FINELY CHOPPED
- 115 G/4 OZ SMOKED SALMON, CUT INTO THIN STRIPS
- 55 G/2 OZ ROCKET
- SALT AND PEPPER
- ½ LEMON, TO GARNISH

1 Bring a large, heavy-based saucepan of lightly salted water to the boil. Add the pasta, return to the boil and cook for 8–10 minutes, or until the pasta is tender but still firm to the bite.

2 Just before the end of the cooking time, heat the olive oil in a heavy-based frying pan. Add the garlic and cook over a low heat for 1 minute, stirring constantly. Do not allow the garlic to brown or it will taste bitter. Add the salmon and rocket. Season to taste with salt and pepper and cook for 1 minute, stirring constantly. Remove the frying pan from the heat.

3 Drain the pasta and transfer to a warmed serving dish. Add the smoked salmon and rocket mixture, toss lightly and serve, garnished with the lemon half.

FISH BAKED **IN SALT**

SERVES 4

INGREDIENTS
- 900 G/2 LB SALT
- 140 G/5 OZ PLAIN FLOUR
- 225 ML/8 FL OZ WATER
- 1 DORADO OR GILTHEAD
  BREAM, ABOUT 1 KG/2 LB 4 OZ,
  GUTTED THROUGH THE GILLS
- 2 LEMON SLICES
- FEW SPRIGS FRESH PARSLEY

1 Preheat the oven to 230°C/450°F/Gas Mark 8. Mix the salt and flour in a bowl and make a well in the middle. Pour in the water to make a thick paste. Set the mixture aside.

2 Push the lemon and parsley into the gill cavity. Use kitchen paper to wipe the fish dry. Cover the fish with the salt paste, using your hands. (It's not necessary to scale the fish before you add the paste, but do take care not to cut yourself.) Place in a roasting tin, making sure the fish is completely covered.

3 Roast the fish in the preheated oven for 30 minutes. Remove from the oven and crack the crust. As you pull the crust back, it should bring the skin with it. Fillet the flesh and serve immediately.

SMOKED SALMON, ASPARAGUS & AVOCADO SALAD

SERVES 4

INGREDIENTS

- 200 G/7 OZ FRESH ASPARAGUS SPEARS
- 1 LARGE RIPE AVOCADO
- 1 TBSP LEMON JUICE
- LARGE HANDFUL FRESH ROCKET LEAVES
- 225 G/8 OZ SMOKED SALMON SLICES
- 1 RED ONION, FINELY SLICED
- 1 TBSP CHOPPED FRESH PARSLEY
- 1 TBSP CHOPPED FRESH CHIVES

DRESSING

- 1 GARLIC CLOVE, CHOPPED
- 4 TBSP EXTRA VIRGIN OLIVE OIL
- 2 TBSP WHITE WINE VINEGAR
- 1 TBSP LEMON JUICE
- PINCH OF SUGAR
- 1 TSP MUSTARD

1 Bring a large saucepan of lightly salted water to the boil. Add the asparagus and cook for 4 minutes, then drain. Refresh under cold running water and drain again. Set aside to cool.

2 To make the dressing, combine all the ingredients in a small bowl and stir together well. Cut the avocado in half lengthways, then remove and discard the stone and skin. Cut the flesh into bite-sized pieces and brush with lemon juice to prevent discoloration.

3 To assemble the salad, arrange the rocket leaves on individual serving plates and top with the asparagus and avocado. Cut the smoked salmon into strips and scatter over the top of the salad, then scatter over the onion and herbs. Drizzle over the dressing and serve.

SMOKED TROUT WITH PEARS

SERVES 4

INGREDIENTS
- 55 G/2 OZ WATERCRESS
- 1 HEAD OF RADICCHIO, TORN INTO PIECES
- 4 SMOKED TROUT FILLETS, SKINNED
- 2 RIPE PEARS, SUCH AS WILLIAMS
- 2 TBSP LEMON JUICE
- 2 TBSP EXTRA VIRGIN OLIVE OIL
- 3 TBSP SOURED CREAM
- 2 TSP CREAMED HORSERADISH
- SALT AND PEPPER
- THINLY SLICED BUTTERED BROWN BREAD, CRUSTS REMOVED, TO SERVE

1 Place the watercress and radicchio in a bowl. Cut the trout fillets into thin strips and add to the bowl. Halve and core the pears, then slice thinly. Place in a separate bowl, add 4 teaspoons of the lemon juice and toss to coat. Add the pears to the salad.

2 To make the dressing, mix the remaining lemon juice and the olive oil together in a bowl, then season to taste with salt and pepper. Pour the dressing over the salad and toss well. Transfer to a large salad bowl.

3 Mix the soured cream and horseradish together in a separate bowl until thoroughly blended, then serve with the salad, together with the buttered bread.

KEDGEREE

SERVES 4

INGREDIENTS

- 450 G/1 LB UNDYED SMOKED HADDOCK, SKINNED
- 2 TBSP OLIVE OIL
- 1 ONION, FINELY CHOPPED
- 1 TSP MILD CURRY PASTE
- 175 G/6 OZ LONG-GRAIN WHITE RICE
- 55 G/2 OZ BUTTER
- 3 HARD-BOILED EGGS
- SALT AND PEPPER
- 2 TBSP CHOPPED FRESH PARSLEY, TO GARNISH

1 Put the fish in a large saucepan and cover with water. Bring the water to the boil, then reduce the heat and simmer for 8–10 minutes until the fish flakes easily.

2 Remove the fish with a slotted spoon and keep warm, reserving the cooking liquid in a jug or bowl.

3 Heat the oil in the pan over a medium heat, add the onion and cook, stirring frequently, for 4 minutes, or until soft. Stir in the curry paste and add the rice.

4 Measure 600 ml/1 pint of the haddock cooking liquid and return to the pan. Bring to a simmer and cover. Cook for 10–12 minutes until the rice is tender and the water has been absorbed. Season to taste with salt and pepper.

5 Flake the fish and add to the pan with the butter. Stir very gently over a low heat until the butter has melted. Chop 2 of the hard-boiled eggs and add to the pan.

6 Turn the kedgeree into a serving dish, slice the remaining egg and use to garnish. Scatter over the chopped parsley and serve immediately.

GRAVADLAX

SERVES 8–12

INGREDIENTS

- 2 SALMON FILLETS, SKIN ON, ABOUT 450 G/1 LB EACH
- 6 TBSP ROUGHLY CHOPPED FRESH DILL
- 115 G/4 OZ SEA SALT
- 50 G/1¾ OZ SUGAR
- 1 TBSP WHITE PEPPERCORNS, ROUGHLY CRUSHED
- LEMON SLICES AND FRESH DILL SPRIGS, TO GARNISH
- 12 SLICES BROWN BREAD, BUTTERED, TO SERVE

1 Rinse the salmon fillets under cold running water and dry with kitchen paper. Put 1 fillet, skin side down, in a non-metallic dish.

2 Mix the dill, sea salt, sugar and peppercorns together in a small bowl. Spread this mixture over the fillet in the dish and put the second fillet, skin side up, on top. Put a plate, the same size as the fish, on top and weigh down with 3–4 food cans.

3 Chill in the refrigerator for 2 days, turning the fish about every 12 hours and basting with any juices that come out of the fish.

4 Remove the salmon from the brine and thinly slice, without slicing the skin, as you would smoked salmon. Garnish with the lemon wedges and dill sprigs. Cut the buttered bread into triangles and serve with the salmon.